FORTRESS • 96

THE FORTRESS OF RHODES 1309–1522

KONSTANTIN NOSSOV

ILLUSTRATED BY BRIAN DELF

Series editor Marcus Cowper

First published in 2010 by Osprey Publishing
Midland House, West Way, Botley, Oxford OX2 0PH, UK
44-02 23rd St, Suite 219, Long Island City, NY 11101, USA
E-mail: info@ospreypublishing.com

ISBN: 978 184603 930 0
E-book ISBN: 978 1 84603 931 7

Editorial by Ilios Publishing Ltd, Oxford, UK (www.iliospublishing.com)
Cartography: Map Studio, Romsey, UK
Page layout by Ken Vail Graphic Design, Cambridge, UK (kvgd.com)
Typset in Myriad and Sabon
Index by Sandra Shotter
Originated by PDQ Media Digital Media Solutions Ltd, UK
Printed in China through Bookbuilders

10 11 12 13 14   10 9 8 7 6 5 4 3 2 1

A CIP catalogue record for this book is available from the British Library.

FOR A CATALOGUE OF ALL BOOKS PUBLISHED BY OSPREY MILITARY
AND AVIATION PLEASE CONTACT:

Osprey Direct, c/o Random House Distribution Center,
400 Hahn Road, Westminster, MD 21157
Email: uscustomerservice@ospreypublishing.com

Osprey Direct, The Book Service Ltd, Distribution Centre,
Colchester Road, Frating Green, Colchester, Essex, CO7 7DW
E-mail: customerservice@ospreypublishing.com

www.ospreypublishing.com

ARTIST'S NOTE

Readers may care to note that the original paintings from which the
colour plates in this book were prepared are available for private sale.
All reproduction copyright whatsoever is retained by the Publishers.
All enquiries should be addressed to:

Brian Delf, 7 Burcot Park, Burcot Abingdon, OX14 3DH, UK

The Publishers regret that they can enter into no correspondence upon
this matter.

THE FORTRESS STUDY GROUP (FSG)

The object of the FSG is to advance the education of the public in the
study of all aspects of fortifications and their armaments, especially
works constructed to mount or resist artillery. The FSG holds an annual
conference in September over a long weekend with visits and evening
lectures, an annual tour abroad lasting about eight days, and an annual
Members' Day.

The FSG journal FORT is published annually, and its newsletter Casemate
is published three times a year. Membership is international. For further
details, please contact:

Website: www.fsgfort.com

Secretary: secretary@fsgfort.com

THE HISTORY OF FORTIFICATION STUDY CENTRE (HFSC)

The History of Fortification Study Centre (HFSC) is an international scientific
research organization that aims to unite specialists in the history of military
architecture from antiquity to the 20th century (including historians, art
historians, archaeologists, architects and those with a military background).
The centre has its own scientific council, which is made up of authoritative
experts who have made an important contribution to the study of
fortification.

The HFSC's activities involve organizing conferences, launching research
expeditions to study monuments of defensive architecture, contributing
to the preservation of such monuments, arranging lectures and special
courses in the history of fortification and producing published works such
as the refereed academic journal Questions of the History of Fortification,
monographs and books on the history of fortification. It also holds a
competition for the best publication of the year devoted to the history
of fortification.

The headquarters of the HFSC is in Moscow, Russia, but the centre is
active in the international arena and both scholars and amateurs from all
countries are welcome to join. More detailed information about the HFSC
and its activities can be found on the website: www.hfsc.3dn.ru

E-mail: ciif-info@yandex.ru

THE WOODLAND TRUST

Osprey Publishing are supporting the Woodland Trust, the UK's leading
woodland conservation charity, by funding the dedication of trees.

EDITOR'S NOTE

Unless otherwise indicated, all images in this book are the property of the
author. All requests should be addressed to: konst-nosov@mtu-net.ru or
konstantin_nossov@yahoo.com.

CONTENTS

THE FORTRESS OF RHODES 1309–1522

INTRODUCTION

Pro Fide [For Faith]

Motto of the Sovereign Military Hospitaller Order of St John of Jerusalem, of Rhodes and of Malta.

The island of Rhodes in the Aegean Sea has been inhabited since the Neolithic period. Excavations show that Greek settlements existed on the island as early as the first half of the 2nd millennium BC. The Minoans appeared here in the 16th century BC, and the Achaeans in the 15th century BC. The 11th century BC saw the arrival of the Dorians, who are responsible for the building of three large cities that prospered during the centuries that followed: Ialysos, Lindos and Kamiros. Lindos was an important naval and mercantile base in the region in the 8th–6th centuries BC. In the late 5th century BC the inhabitants of Ialysos, Lindos and Kamiros decided to combine their efforts and build a new city, which was founded on the northern extremity of the island in 408 BC and called Rhodes. According to the Athenian architect Hippodamus, the city had a regular layout, a good water supply and a good

Remains of a tower that belonged to Rhodes' Hellenistic walls. Only some foundations survive of the formidable antique walls that once encircled the city, enrapturing its visitors. Unfortunately, even the line of these walls cannot be followed everywhere.

Gate to a barbican at St Paul Gate. High vertical slits indicate that a drawbridge used to be fastened here.

sewer system. Comfortable harbours and an advantageous position on trade routes from East to West were conducive to the city's prosperity. By the late 4th century BC it had acquired formidable defensive walls, which successfully withstood the siege of the army of Demetrius Poliorcetes in 305/04 BC. The walls of Rhodes were an excellent example of a fortification from the Hellenistic era, and Philon of Byzantium admired them in the mid-3rd century BC. In 227/26 BC the walls suffered considerably in an earthquake, but were restored owing to the financial and technical support of many Greek city-states. Rhodes was later owned by the Romans, and then by the Byzantines, who built a fortress here. In the Middle Ages Rhodes lost the power and magnificence it had boasted in antiquity. It was only the Order of St John that breathed new life into the city and made it shine again.

By the time they settled on the island of Rhodes, the Hospitallers already had great experience in building fortifications. The maintenance of castles within crusader states had become a great problem for Christian rulers, who frequently lacked manpower. They were therefore only too glad to pass on responsibility for the most vulnerable castles to military orders capable of protecting them. In exchange for the obligation to maintain

Main wall of the English (originally Aragon) Post. The rectangular tower on a massive socle was first a detached structure connected to the main wall by a small bridge, and had a battlemented parapet. It was later joined to the wall (which has a different type of masonry), and the battlemented parapet was replaced with a slanting one suitable for artillery.

Loophole in the shape of a so-called inverted keyhole, at the barbican at St Paul Gate. These loopholes were primarily designed for shooting with firearms, while a circular opening at the bottom is evidence that a small cannon could also be used to shoot through it.

fortifications and keep the garrison, the Hospitallers were frequently presented with whole castles or parts of a castle (for instance, a tower and a barbican in the Kerak in Moab). The wealth of the Order grew, and by 1160 it was already rich enough to buy castles outright. By the time of the conflict with Saladin the Order had 27 castles, and all in all over 30 castles passed through Hospitaller hands at different times. No wonder that, being the owners of such a great number of castles, they became expert in fortification. Louis IX is known to have asked for the Hospitallers' advice about fortifying Caesarea in 1251.

The Order of St John was an international organization that had territorial possessions (priories) in many Western European countries. Consequently, its members were divided into national communities known as langues. The langues were first mentioned in 1206. By the time it arrived in Rhodes, the Order counted seven langues: Aragon (which comprised all the knights coming from the Iberian Peninsula), Auvergne, England (including Scotland and Ireland), France, Germany, Italy and Provence. In 1461 the faction of Castile–Portugal detached from the langue of Aragon, bringing the total up to eight. At the time of Henry VIII the langue of England was eliminated and the Bavarian langue appeared instead. Only a citizen of one of those nations could apply for membership of the Order. Within the city of Rhodes, each langue owned an inn, which was the place of assembly for all brothers of the same community. The Rhodian garrison comprised representatives of all langues, and each langue was given a section of the city to defend. The division of the city defences in this manner stimulated rivalry between members of different nations, with each langue trying to excel the others in bravery and steadfastness. Brother-knights and brother-sergeants-at-arms were the elite of the Order's troops, while the majority of its army, as well as the garrison of the fortresses, consisted of mercenaries.

Like other lands belonging to the Order, the island of Rhodes was divided into several districts (*castellanies*). Each district had a castle under the command of a Hospitaller captain (*castellan*), who was a war-hardened knight as a rule. He commanded several brothers-in-arms, mercenaries and local militias. Rhodes boasted over 20 castles, excluding watchtowers. In case of danger these castles could give shelter to the local population. However, except for the city-fortress of Rhodes and a few other fortresses (Lindos, Pheraclos, Horio in Kalymnos and Platanos in Leros) most of the castles were rather poorly fortified. They could offer protection from pirates plundering on the coasts of the Aegean Sea, but were unable to withstand a full siege. Therefore, when threatened with a serious invasion the inhabitants of Rhodes and the other islands belonging to the Order were evacuated to the city.

According to the statutes of 1311 and 1314, the permanent garrison of the fortress was to consist of 500 cavalrymen and 1,000 infantrymen. There were not enough people to meet this total however, so in 1313 the Order issued a decree that all westerners who settled on Rhodes and served as soldiers or sailors were to be given land and pensions. In 1340 the garrison of Rhodes consisted of 200 Knights Hospitallers, 50 mounted brother-sergeants, 50 mounted secular men-at-arms and 1,000 infantrymen. To withstand great sieges the Rhodian garrison was increased at the expense of garrisons from other Hospitaller fortresses and sailors from their ships and galleys, as well as mercenaries and volunteers from Europe. In case of an attack, the local Greek population was also engaged in defending the city and was provided with weapons from the Order's armouries.

CHRONOLOGY

408 BC	The city of Rhodes is founded.
c.1080	A small brotherhood is established in Jerusalem (at the time belonging to the Saracens) to tend sick, injured and indigent pilgrims in hospital.
1099	The crusaders seize Jerusalem in the course of the First Crusade. The brotherhood of Hospitallers evolves into a knightly order, with Blessed Gerard (Gerard Thom), the founder of the brotherhood, becoming its first master.
1120	After the death of Blessed Gerard, the Order of St John is headed by Master Raymond du Puy. Under him the Order is transformed from a monastic to a military order.
1136	King Fulk of Jerusalem bestows the castle Bait Gibrin on the Order.
1142	Count Raymond of Tripoli presents the Order with his two frontier fortresses – the castles Montferrand and Hosn al-Akrad (Crac de Chevaliers).
1144	The Order of St John obtains three more castles (Felicium, Lacum and Castellum Bochee) in the county of Tripoli.
1160s	The Order of St John begins to acquire castles on its own.
1168	The Hospitallers buy the castle of Belvoir.
1186	The Order is presented with the castle of Marqab.
1187	Saladin takes Jerusalem and the castle of Bait Gibrin. The Hospitallers have to withdraw their headquarters from Jerusalem and later move it to Acre.
1189	After a drawn-out siege the Knights of St John lose the castle of Belvoir.
1271	Sultan Baybars of Egypt takes Crac de Chevaliers by assault.
1285	After a bloody siege Baybars seizes Marqab.
1291	The siege and fall of Acre. The crusaders are now deprived of almost all their property in the Latin East. The Hospitallers transfer their headquarters to Cyprus.
1291–1309	The Order of St John is based on Cyprus.
1305–17	Grand Master Foulques de Villaret.
1306	The Hospitallers begin their invasion of Rhodes.
1309	The city of Rhodes is seized, and the island is finally occupied by the Knights of St John. Their headquarters is moved from Cyprus to Rhodes.
1310–12	The Turks vainly attempt to drive the Hospitallers away from Rhodes.
1313	The Order of St John takes possession of the neighbouring islands of Karpathos and Kassos but following a conflict with Venice has to give them up in 1315.
1314	The Hospitallers occupy the island of Kos. They lose it several years later and acquire it again in 1336.
1317	Revolt of the Knights of St John resentful of the luxurious lifestyle and despotism of Grand Master Foulques de Villaret. Brother-knights proclaim Maurice de Pagnac their new Grand Master.
1318/19	The Turks make new unsuccessful attempts to banish the Knights from Rhodes.

1319	The Pope interferes with internal conflict in the Order. Both Grand Masters (Foulques de Villaret and Maurice de Pagnac) retire. Hélion de Villeneuve becomes the new Grand Master. The same year sees the Hospitallers take back the island of Leros, where insurgent Greeks had slaughtered the Order's garrison.
1319–46	Grand Master Hélion de Villeneuve.
1346–53	Grand Master Dieudonné de Gozon.
1353–55	Grand Master Pierre de Corneillan.
1355–65	Grand Master Roger de Pins.
1365–74	Grand Master Raymond Berenger.
1374–76	Grand Master Robert de Juilly.
1376–96	Grand Master Juan Fernandez de Heredia.
1396–1421	Grand Master Philibert de Naillac.
1421–37	Grand Master Antonio Fluvian (de la Riviere).
1437–54	Grand Master Jean de Lastic.
1440	The Sultan of Egypt unsuccessfully tries to seize Rhodes.
1440–89	The Order builds a stone hospital in Rhodes, which has survived until the present day.
1444	Another attempt on the fortress of Rhodes is made by Egyptians. A 40-day siege accompanied by numerous assaults fails to gain victory for the Egyptians, and they withdraw.
1454–61	Grand Master Jacques de Milly.
1461–67	Grand Master Piero Raimundo Zacosta.
1467–76	Grand Master Giovanni Battista Orsini.
1476–1503	Grand Master Pierre d'Aubusson.
1480	Unsuccessful Turkish siege of Rhodes.
1503–12	Grand Master Emery d'Amboise.
1512–13	Grand Master Guy de Blanchefort.
1513–21	Grand Master Fabrizio del Carretto.
1521–34	Grand Master Philippe Villiers de l'Isle Adam.
1522	A bloody siege of Rhodes results in the Knights' capitulation to the Turks, who now become the owners of Rhodes. After several years of wandering the Knights of St John settle on Malta (1530).

DESIGN AND DEVELOPMENT

History of the building of the Rhodes Fortress

Strange as it may seem, Rhodian fortifications have little in common with the strongholds of the Knights of St John in the Latin East. This may probably be accounted for by the fact that at first the Hospitallers did not have to build powerful fortifications on the island, whereas the conception of fortifications had changed greatly by the time the need to build them occurred.

For some time after they moved to Rhodes, the Hospitallers were content with the Byzantine fortifications of the city. The explanation for this lies in the absence of any serious danger; a few weak and unsuccessful Turkish attempts to drive the Order out of Rhodes in 1310–12 and 1318/19 were followed by more than a century of peaceful existence.

The Byzantine city occupied a small part of the area covered by its antique predecessor, and the northern part of the Hospitallers' city. As the site lacked any protective relief features, trust was placed in the man-made fortifications. The Knights spent the first half of the 14th century restoring and extending the Byzantine fortifications to the south and east in order to enclose an expanding

Wall-walk on the barbican at St Paul Gate. On the right of the loophole, in the merlon and in the butt-end of the merlon above a stairway, there are stone juts to place torches in. To detect a surprise attack at night the patrol on the walls should have torches at hand.

suburb and protect a vitally important port. Ludolf de Suchen, who visited Rhodes under Grand Master Hélion de Villeneuve (1319–46), noted the Order's activity in building city walls. De Villeneuve's coat of arms (together with that of Orsini's) above the south-east gate of Collachium (the old town) shows that the work was completed in the first half of the 14th century. Grand Master Dieudonné de Gozon (1346–53) repaired the harbour mole and encircled the port with fortifications. Grand Master Juan Fernandez de Heredia (1376–96) repaired and further strengthened the walls protecting the harbour.

It was, however, in the early 15th century when the Order set about to work earnestly on the city's fortifications. Grand Master Philibert de Naillac (1396–1421) continued to fortify the harbour and supplied the tip of the harbour mole with a great tower named after him. His successor, Grand Master Antonio Fluvian (1421–37), paid particular attention to the protection of the city on the mainland side. He is known for certain to have erected such key structures as St George, St Athanassios and St John Towers, as well as a double wall in the Post of Spain (which was English at that time). It was probably under Grand Master Fluvian that the whole of the mainland side acquired a double wall fortified with towers, with the inner wall higher than

Tower of the Virgin Mary erected in 1441/42 under Grand Master Jean de Lastic. It was the main tower of the then Aragon Post. This may explain why it was built, like the other towers of the post, in the Spanish–Portuguese 'albarra' style (i.e. as a free-standing structure). It is protected by the bulwark of England, which, like the bulwark of Provence, is not connected to the main fortress wall.

the outer one. The fortifications were evidently built on the model of the walls of Constantinople.

In the early 15th century, chiefly in the time of Grand Master Antonio Fluvian, himself a Spaniard, Hospitaller fortifications experienced a Spanish–Portuguese influence. It is reflected in the turrets (bartizans) projecting outwards from the corners of some towers. The Naillac Tower is one example – although it is now destroyed it can be seen in the Caoursin manuscript. The Spanish–Portuguese influence could also be seen in detached towers that were brought forwards and connected with the wall by easily removed bridges (the so-called 'albarra' style). The latter structure had a number of advantages: the power of flanking fire from the towers was increased, the falling of a tower no longer caused the falling of the curtain and vice versa, and if a tower was seized by the enemy, it could easily be isolated. Several similar towers can be seen today in the Aragon (later English) Post.

In the same period the spread of gunpowder artillery began to alter the Rhodian fortifications and caused the appearance of round towers and gun loopholes. It should be noted that both innovations were introduced in the Order's fortifications comparatively late. Round towers had been known since antiquity and spread throughout Western European countries shortly after the Crusades. Loopholes for cannon (shaped like an inverted keyhole) appeared, for instance, in England in the 1380s. The fortress of Rhodes, however, saw the first loopholes for cannon in St George Tower built between 1421 and 1437.

Grand Master Jean de Lastic (1437–54) strengthened the north-western corner of the fortress. Here, side by side with the Grand Masters' Palace a whole complex of fortifications was built, which included the Cannon and St Anthony Gates and ended with the polygonal Battery of the Olives in the north. Now the Grand Masters' Palace was safely protected on the mainland side of the post, for which the Grand Masters were responsible. Moreover, Jean de Lastic reconstructed and strengthened the fortifications in the German, Auvergne and English (then Aragon) Posts. In 1441/42 he had the Tower of the Virgin Mary erected in the latter post. It was also at this time that the Tower of the Windmills was built on the eastern mole for the protection of the harbour.

Gate in the pentagonal bulwark-barbican in front of the Tower of St John, at the Post of Provence. The barbican was apparently constructed under Grand Master Piero Raimundo Zacosta (1461–67).

Grand Master Jacques de Milly (1454–61) was the first to start building polygonal bulwarks in front of the old towers of the city wall. His coat of arms is evidence of the creation of a triangular bulwark in the Post of Provence.

Fortifications in the French Post, extending from the Grand Masters' Palace to the harbour, were built under Grand Master Piero Raimundo Zacosta (1461–67). To the north of these fortifications, on an old mole, he erected St Nicholas Tower. This Grand Master also had pentagonal bulwark-barbicans constructed in front of St John and St George Towers.

Grand Master Giovanni Battista Orsini (1467–76) modernized fortifications along the harbour. He also widened the ditch in front of the walls on the mainland side and built short cross-walls to connect the free-standing towers with the main wall.

Grand Master Pierre d'Aubusson (1476–1503), hero of the siege of Rhodes in 1480 and a gifted military engineer, carried out the most substantial work in fortifying the city. At first his activity was urged on by feverish preparations for a siege, and afterwards by the destruction caused by the siege of 1480 and the next year's earthquake. It was during the siege of 1480 when Rhodes was exposed to powerful artillery fire for the first time, revealing imperfections in the fortifications of the city. It was also clear that the Turks would not give up their attempts to drive the Order away from the island, so as soon as the siege was lifted Grand Master Pierre d'Aubusson set to work on restoring and strengthening the fortifications. His coat of arms, to be seen on the city walls in more than 50 places, is evidence of this Grand Master's enormous building activity. Pierre d'Aubusson considerably increased the thickness of the main wall, which became 5m or even 12m thick in some sections. This allowed the accommodation of powerful cannon on its wall-walk as well as the speedy transfer of troops. He introduced another innovation by considerably widening the ditch and changing the outer profile of the fortress bulwark on the mainland side. He did this by turning the counterscarp of the original ditch at the posts of England, Spain, Italy and Grand Masters into massive advanced earthworks (*tenailles*). Formidable polygonal bulwarks were built in front of the main towers of the posts of Auvergne, England, Aragon and Provence by 1489. All these outworks differed in height and shape, which suggests that the Hospitallers experimented in search of optimal protection. Besides this, to increase defence capacity on the mainland side some of the gates were blocked up and others were strengthened. Nor did Pierre d'Aubusson neglect waterside defences: the Tower of the Windmills and St Nicholas Tower were reconstructed and fortified and turned into forts, and the Sea Gate was either built or rebuilt. Grand Master Emery d'Amboise (1503–12) built a gate, named after him, in the earthen outwork in front of Anthony Gate and the Grand Masters' Palace.

Fabrizio del Carretto (1513–21) was the last Grand Master to have time to alter or add anything to the fortifications of the city. He built a semicircular bulwark in front of the Tower of Italy, and low structures to enable flanking fire into the ditch (*caponiers*). He also changed the older parapet on the walls for a new one of rounded shape designed for mounting artillery, and considerably increased the thickness of the main wall on the mainland side.

The nationality of a Grand Master seriously influenced the strengthening of this or that sector of the fortress of Rhodes. That was a consequence of the division of the fortress defences into langues according to nationality. For instance, Grand Master Pierre d'Aubusson, an Auvergnat, substantially fortified the whole city, but had the most powerful bastion (St George Bastion)

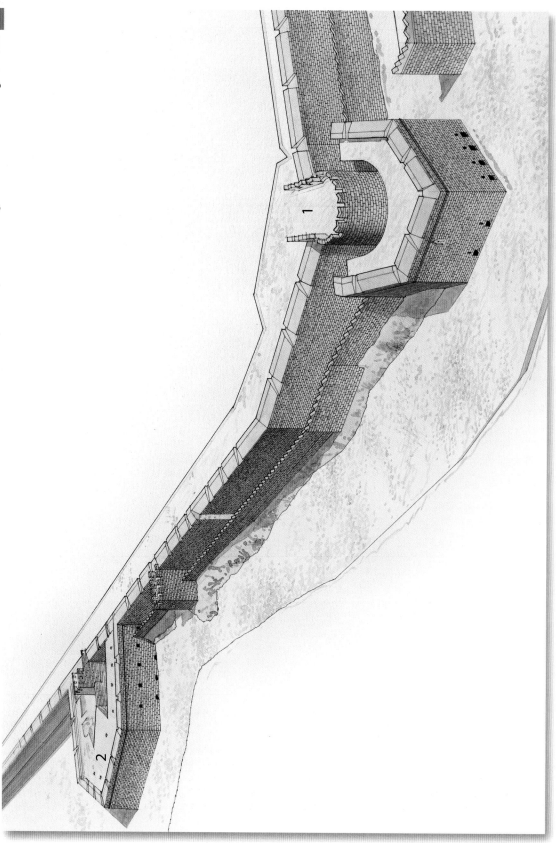

Fortifications of the posts of Spain and Auvergne on the eve of the siege of 1522

built at the Auvergne Post. The French Grand Master Emery d'Amboise constructed the formidable d'Amboise Gate in the French Post. The Italian Fabrizio del Carretto did a great deal in fortifying the city as a whole, but paid special attention to the Italian Post, building a semicircular outwork there.

Artillery fortification, in search of new forms

Western European fortification underwent startling changes in the late 15th and early 16th centuries, with Rhodian fortifications playing a remarkable part in the process. Created at the beginning of the 14th century, cannon were at first too ineffective to make a noticeable impact on fortifications. In the 15th century, however, their power grew swiftly and soon surpassed the power of any catapult device. Gigantic bombards came into being, which could shoot enormous projectiles weighing several hundred kilograms. By the end of the 15th century more effective granular powder was invented, and stone cannon balls gradually gave way to cast-iron ones. As early as the late 15th century, cannon could easily break the walls of medieval castles. This fact roused engineers in all countries to search for new forms of fortification capable of withstanding this terrible weapon.

View of the Spanish (originally English) Post from the Tower of Spain. Earlier fortifications comprising a double wall were erected at the time of Grand Master Antonio Fluvian (1421–37). Later, owing to the efforts made by Pierre d'Aubusson, a formidable earthwork *tenaille* was built.

A **FORTIFICATIONS OF THE POSTS OF SPAIN AND AUVERGNE ON THE EVE OF THE SIEGE OF 1522**

The Spanish Post stretches from the Tower of Spain (1) to the Tower of the Virgin Mary. During the siege of 1480 the sector was under the charge of the English knights. Later the posts of England and Aragon changed places, and in 1522 the sector was defended by the Spanish knights. Since that time the tower has been called the Tower of Spain. In 1489 a bulwark of a slightly distorted pentagonal shape was constructed in front of the Tower of Spain.

In 1421–31 the Hospitallers built their first fortifications on the site where St George Bastion (2) – the main stronghold of the Post of Auvergne – was later to be erected. Those first defences comprised a rectangular tower and a gate. The mid-15th century saw a pentagonal bulwark-barbican constructed here, and in 1486 under Grand Master Pierre d'Aubusson a gate was blocked up and a bastion of a slightly irregular pentagonal form built in front of the tower. St George Bastion became the most powerful stronghold of the Fortress of Rhodes and one of the earliest pentagonal bastions in history. It was an excellent gun platform. Two-tier mural galleries with gun ports were made in the flanks of the bastion to enable the defenders to sweep the ditch with flanking fire. An underground countermine gallery began from the bastion and ran under the ditch.

Fortifications by the Gate of St John seen from the east, at the Post of Provence. Several lines of defences provided for several tiers of fire. Vertical slits with square and round apertures at the bottom were designed for cannon manned by two people. These are early examples of artillery loopholes.

While securely protecting the walls from escalade, the high curtains and towers of medieval castles were excellent targets for cannon. Their height was brought down and the height of towers was brought level with that of the curtains. The ditch became deeper and its sides acquired a stone facing. The walls grew thicker, often owing to an earthen embankment added on the inner side of the wall; the outer side of curtains and towers was sometimes covered with turf to soften the impact of cannon balls. Merlons and machicolations were gradually given up as they could easily be broken off by cannon balls, when fragments could inflict serious losses on the defenders. The medieval battlemented parapet was replaced by a thicker rounded one, with wide funnel-shaped embrasures for cannon.

The changes in fortification design were not confined to these minor alterations, however. Entirely new forms of fortification were needed to resist artillery fire. It is generally accepted that it was Italian engineers who were responsible for turning the medieval castle into the bastioned fortress of the Renaissance period. Let us trace the changes in fortification design in the late 15th to early 16th centuries.

During the last three decades of the 15th century Italy was the first to experiment with bastioned forms. Ideas were innovated by Francesco di Giorgio Martini and the brothers Giuliano and Antonio da Sangallo. In 1474 Francesco di Giorgio Martini set out to build the fortress of Sassocorvaro, and the fortress of San Leo in 1479. In 1483–86 Giuliano da Sangallo together with Baccio Pontelli completely rebuilt a fortress in Ostia. Formidable round squat towers practically no higher than the curtains were a characteristic feature of all these fortresses. These had two advantages: first, they allowed the transfer of troops along the wall-walk with much greater speed; and second, they removed the threat of a high tower, easily damaged by artillery, falling down on the curtain and blocking the movement of troops in this section. The towers and walls of the fortresses in San Leo and Ostia still had machicolations, but at the same time they were already adjusted to accommodate artillery.

Widely used squat round towers were the first response to the growing artillery power. Unlike rectangular ones, round towers were less subject to destruction by artillery as a ball rarely hit them at a right angle; it usually made contact at a tangent, which reduced the damage caused. Still, a circular tower had a serious disadvantage: there was dead ground uncontrolled even by flanking fire from the part of the tower projecting farthest towards the enemy (although the dead ground in the case of a circular tower was much smaller than that of a rectangular one). Therefore, the next step was developing a fortification that faced the enemy at an acute angle. Now, enemy cannon balls would slide along the surface of a fortification without doing serious damage to it, and at the same time there would be no dead ground at all. That is how the bastion form was born.

These innovations did not spring up at a moment's notice, though. The fortresses of Sassocorvaro and Ostia provide an opportunity to see engineers experimenting with the new fortification structure in the form of projections with their acute angles turned in the direction of the enemy. In Sassocorvaro the projection was of a triangular shape, and in Ostia it was already pentagonal, thus being an early form of bastion which might be called a 'protobastion'. Judging by his drawings created between 1507 and 1510, Leonardo da Vinci saw a somewhat different way of meeting this challenge: his low round towers were put on a high, formidable socle broadening at the bottom. The socle was polyhedral, with an acute angle jutting in the direction of the enemy.

In 1487 Giuliano da Sangallo made a plan for the modernization of the fortress Poggio Imperiale, consisting of ten bastions. In 1492 Antonio da Sangallo set about fortifying the Pope's residence – the Castel Sant'Angelo (Castle of St Angel) in Rome. He modernized the outer round towers and put low heptagonal protobastions in front of them. In the years 1493–1502 the fortress of Sarzanello was built, which comprised three squat circular towers not rising higher than the walls, one central square tower and a triangular protobastion. In 1494, again for Pope Alexander VI, Antonio da Sangallo began to build a small pentagonal fortress called Civitacastellana; it had four bastions, one round tower and a keep. Civitacastellana became the first fortress completely free of machicolations.

Thus, by the early 16th century the development of the arrowhead-shaped bastion was completed. The first half of the 16th century saw bastioned fortifications built everywhere in Italy: in 1501–03 a small bastioned fort was built in Nettuno, near Rome; in 1533–37 a fort of bastioned layout was built in Florence; in 1535–49 a compact fortress of Aquila with four bastions was built and in 1544 polygonal fortifications with bastioned fronts began to be erected around the whole town of Lucca.

From the early 16th century a general tendency could be observed in European fortifications: they were sinking into the ground. A fortress was built in such a way that only an insignificant part of it (half or less than half of the height of the walls) was visible above the surface. The rest of the fortress sat below ground level. This was achieved by surrounding the fortress with a deep and wide ditch, so to a besieging enemy the fortress appeared to be embedded in the ground. As a result, enemy fire could damage only the upper part of the fortifications, while in assault, besiegers were still faced with high walls as they had first to get down to the bottom of the ditch before starting their attack.

The observations mentioned above are general tendencies. It would be a mistake to believe that medieval castles had disappeared overnight. Stone fortifications were very expensive at all times. The construction of a stone tower could sometimes cost a whole fortune equal to the price of a small estate. Therefore, new forms of fortification were mainly applied to newly erected or radically reconstructed fortresses. As for most of the old castles, efforts were made to adjust them to new requirements through minimal changes – making walls lower and thicker and building outworks involving new construction techniques became common practice. Nevertheless, even fortresses erected 'from scratch' in the early 16th century were not necessarily polygonal,

Multi-tier fortifications at the border of the Spanish and English Posts, at the junction of a Spanish *tenaille* and English bulwark. The arrangement provided for the possibility of conducting multi-tier fire and controlling the ditch in every direction.

nor did they always contain bastions. In Italy, for instance, circular squat towers (not bastions) were built in Rocca Maggiore at Assisi in 1538 and Cortona in 1543. English fortification methods went in their own direction, and the 1540s saw the construction of a number of the so-called castles of Henry VIII, which were characterized by fortifications that were rounded instead of angled.

The development of artillery fortification in Rhodes and Italy examined above proves that Rhodian fortification was quite advanced for its time. Some elements, for instance protobastions in the form of pentagonal bulwark-barbicans, came into being in Rhodes before they appeared in Italy. Also, the classical pattern of bastion – the Bastion of St George (1496) – was developed here at least simultaneously with Italian examples. The architect of the late 15th-century Rhodian fortifications is unknown to us. The only engineer of that time we have any information about is the German Georg Frappan ('Mastrogiorgios' or Master George). At first he worked for the Turks, but then, during the siege of 1480, deserted to the defenders of Rhodes. For some time Master George was in command of a battery of cannon, but then he was accused of treacherous contact with the Turks and was hanged. Nobody knows whether he was guilty or not, as he pleaded

The outer gate leading to the bulwark at the Gate of St John, at the Post of Provence. A course of double moulding separating the upper vertical part of the wall from the lower widening one is characteristic of Pierre d'Aubusson's work. The Grand Master's coat of arms can be seen above the gate alongside that of the Order of St John and a relief of St John the Baptist.

guilty only under torture. It is clear, however, that he took no part in building the fortifications. The man who was probably responsible for the innovations in Rhodian fortification was called Pierre d'Aubusson. Before he became Grand Master in 1476 he held the post of 'Provediteur des Fortifications' and is known to have been an experienced military engineer. It is a fact however that as early as the beginning of the 16th century the building of Rhodian fortifications was carried out with the assistance of Italian engineers: Bartholino de Castilion worked for the Order of St John for several years from 1502 and took part in the construction of fortifications not only in Rhodes but also on Kos and at Bodrum; Basilio dalla Scuola di Vicenza, Emperor Maximilian's personal military engineer, worked in Rhodes in 1519–21; Mastro Zuenio (Gioeni) worked there in 1520 and Gabriele Tadini da Martinengo and Gerolamo Bartolucci were on Rhodes during the siege of 1522. In 1521, on his return from Rhodes, Mastro Zuenio made a wax model of the fortress for Pope Leo X. The model was very accurate and reflected the latest achievements in the fortification of Rhodes: polygonal and semicircular outworks, the addition of *caponiers* and new shapes for parapets and gun embrasures. It is also known that at the request of Pope Alexander VI (1492–1503) the Hospitaller Knight Frá Antonio di S. Martino participated in the building of polygonal outworks in front of the corner towers of the Castel Sant'Angelo in Rome. The similarity of these protobastions to the Rhodian ones is so obvious that even today scholars argue which fortress was original and influenced the other. Taking into consideration such close connections between Rhodes and Italy, it is not surprising that progressive ideas were quickly realized in the fortifications of both states.

Builders of fortifications and building methods

From 1475 onwards two knights were to inspect Rhodian castles and watchtowers every two years. The Council of the Order was to decide whether to build new fortifications or keep up the old ones. It was also to appoint a competent military engineer who would carry on construction work. Subordinate to him was the foreman, usually a local craftsman, who supervised the fulfilment of the engineer's instructions. Under the foreman were master masons, who were each at the head of a team of labourers, slaves and skilled craftsmen. Master masons (*muratores*) were often local Greeks. For instance we know from inscriptions that the Greeks Manolis Kountis ('*protomaistro murador*') and Giorgios Singan ('*murator et protomagister*') were responsible for the erection of certain parts of the walls of the Rhodian fortress.

Native labourers and slaves carried out the bulk of unqualified labour. The slaves, whom the Hospitallers called *argodolati*, were charged with the hardest work. The travellers D. Trevisan and J. Thenaud, who visited Rhodes early in the 16th century, watched 100 Muslim slaves toiling at the city's fortifications. Immediately before the siege of 1522 the Grand Master ordered three fourths of the city slaves, belonging both to the Order and to private owners, to be sent to work strengthening the city's fortifications.

The masonry of the defensive walls of the city of Rhodes built at the time of the Order differed noticeably from both the earlier Byzantine city fortifications and most of the other Hospitallers' fortresses (on the island of Rhodes as well as on other islands). Byzantine fortifications of the city and the Order's less significant fortresses were laid from roughly polished and poorly cut stones, or even rubble, with the interim filled with small stones, tiles and a considerable amount of mortar as a rule. In contrast to this masonry, the defensive walls

Profile of the fortress defences on the mainland side in 1480 and 1522. The defences were subjected to considerable modernization between the first and second sieges of the city of Rhodes. The main wall was made much thicker, and the counterscarp and glacis of the original ditch in the posts of England, Spain, Italy and Grand Masters became a thick, stretched earthwork (*tenaille*) preceded by another ditch.

of the Hospitallers' Rhodes were built from rectangular blocks of regular shape (ashlar masonry) made from yellowish local sandstone. The blocks were mostly placed in courses of equal height (isodomic masonry). Different kinds of laying can be seen in different places: the blocks may all be laid as headers or all as stretchers, or stretchers and headers may alternate in a single course ('header-and-stretcher courses'), or courses of headers may alternate with courses of stretchers ('alternate header/stretcher courses'). Blocks were usually so well fitted to each other that only a small amount of mortar was needed.

The fortifications of Rhodes are adorned with numerous coats of arms of the Grand Masters who created or reconstructed certain sectors of the fortress. These coats of arms are very helpful in dating fortifications. Moreover, in some sectors a course of double molding (a horizontal stone belt) can be seen, which usually separates the upper vertical part of the wall from the lower broadening one. This type of moulding is characteristic of the work of Pierre d'Aubusson.

THE PRINCIPLES OF DEFENCE

The modern city of Rhodes has inherited features from various epochs – an ancient city, a Byzantine town and, most significantly of all, the city of the Order of St John. The latter left the city the greatest number of monuments. Its impressive defences are first on the list. They were not, however, erected all at the same time. In the late 15th to early 16th centuries, on the threshold of the siege of 1522, earlier defences were considerably fortified and modernized, and were skilfully incorporated into the general defensive system. Since 1522 the fortifications of the city of Rhodes have been preserved nearly intact. Today, therefore, the Fortress of Rhodes presents us with complex layers of fortifications dating from different periods.

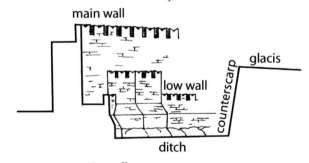

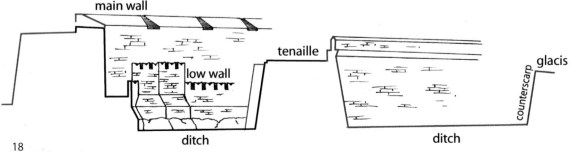

The main wall of the English (originally Aragon) Post is preceded by a long and thick earthen stone-faced *tenaille*, which formed another level of defence and protected the main wall from direct artillery fire.

Each period has left its characteristic traces and these will be singled out for examination alongside those of the individual features of the fortifications.

Profile of defences and general principles of defence

The profile of the fortress defences on the mainland side changed greatly between 1480 and 1522. Earth was added on the inside of the main wall to make it substantially thicker. A complicated system of outworks emerged in front of the curtains and towers to provide for multi-tier and enfilade fire commanding the ditch. The ditch itself became much wider and the counterscarp of the original ditch was turned into thick stretched earthworks (*tenailles*) in some sectors (the posts of England, Spain, Italy and Grand Masters). These earthworks formed one more defensive line and protected the main fortifications of the city from enemy artillery fire. Open at the rear, they could not be used as a bridgehead by the enemy if seized.

The outer side of the ditch was furnished with a glacis – a low embankment of earth sloping gradually away from the fortress. A glacis had two important functions: owing to its flat surface cleared of trees and bushes it turned the attackers into excellent targets, but a much more important consideration was that it protected the lower part of the main *enceinte* from besiegers' artillery fire. Enemy artillerymen could see only the parapet on the walls and towers together with the cannon accommodated there. Meanwhile, on reaching the

The Tower of Italy viewed from the glacis. Owing to the sloping surface of the glacis and the general embedded nature of the defensive walls in the ditch, the fortifications were mostly concealed from enemy artillerymen. Only the upper part of the defences was exposed to a direct artillery fire. Meanwhile, assaulting troops represented an excellent target on the glacis (its surface was specially flattened and cleared of trees and bushes), and on reaching the foot of the glacis they found themselves facing a deep ditch and the high walls of the main *enceinte*.

counterscarp, enemy units in assault found themselves facing a deep and wide ditch and the high walls of the main *enceinte* towering beyond it.

The mainland walls traced a broken, zigzagged line. Towers placed at projecting angles and faced with formidable bulwarks were key points of defence here. The walls between these strongholds were either straight or concave. With this design, flanking fire could easily be brought to bear upon the sectors between strongholds. The latter were 200–350m apart, and cannon could command the space between them with fire from one or both of the strongholds.

The profile of the sea walls remained practically unchanged between the two sieges. Fortifications were less powerful here and had no outworks. Only the towers on the moles protruding far into the sea – the Tower of the Windmills and St Nicholas Tower – were fortified and turned into forts in this period.

Main *enceinte*

The defensive walls of Rhodes erected by the Knights of St John stretched for about 4km. Before 1480 they were comparatively thin and resembled the walls of medieval castles. They survive almost intact in less important sectors – along the perimeter of the commercial port (Castile Post) and in some small sectors of the French and Italian posts, which also look towards the sea.

Fortifications on the more vulnerable mainland side, from somewhere near d'Amboise Gate up to the Italian Post, underwent great changes between 1480 and 1522. Under Grand Masters Pierre d'Aubusson and Fabrizio del Carretto an earthen bank was added to the walls to make them considerably thicker – instead of 4m they now became 12m thick on the mainland side. To preserve outer defences the wall was enlarged on the inside. This required the pulling down of some houses in the city. In September 1520 the citizens were paid 4,104 fiorini in compensation.

The main *enceinte* on the mainland side consists of two defensive lines, with a higher and more powerful inner wall overlooking the outer one. However, the latter is not separated from the former, as in Constantinople for instance. In Rhodes, the space between them was filled with earth up to the parapet level of the outer wall, which added to the thickness and formidableness of the lower part of the main wall. In some sectors the outer wall was strengthened with rectangular towers, which have retained their original appearance.

These two rectangular towers interrupting an inner wall near the Gate of St Paul are the oldest form of Hospitaller fortification that have survived. Built in 1377–96, they have cruciform loopholes and the coat of arms of Grand Master Juan Fernandez de Heredia.

The earliest towers in Rhodes were all rectangular without exception. The oldest of those preserved date from 1377–96. They are two of the towers on the northern side of the fortifications near St Paul Gate. Seen on them is the coat of arms of Grand Master Juan Fernandez de Heredia. The towers are supplied with cruciform loopholes. Rhodian fortification began to adopt round towers in the early 15th century. Almost all the towers, rectangular as well as round, are furnished with *talus*: a broadening of their lower part.

If wall-towers built in the early 15th century were often detached from the wall and only connected to it by small bridges, this principle was given up by the end of the century. With the growth of artillery power, stronger links with the wall were needed. Short cross-walls emerged between freestanding towers and the wall. The masonry of the cross-walls is noticeably unlike that of the wall, so it is not difficult to know which towers used to be detached structures.

Wall-walk of the outer, low wall by St Athanassios Gate. Like other towers of the English Post (originally the Aragon Post), this tower was at first a free-standing structure connected with the wall by small bridges, but was later joined to the *enceinte* by stone walls.

Fortifications built on the extremities of the moles – the Tower of the Windmills and St Nicholas Tower – are of particular interest. Originally, before 1480, the fortifications there were isolated towers. Because of their isolation, the towers needed particularly strong protection. The problem was solved through a curious architectural device – a small turret with a spiral staircase inside was built next to each main tower, and the entrance to the main tower was placed on the first floor, accessed via a small drawbridge thrown out to the staircase-turret. After 1480 both of these towers were encircled in outworks and made into forts.

The gate was always the most difficult defence element. Before 1480 the fortress of Rhodes had five gates on the mainland side (St Anthony, St George, St Athanassios, St John and Acandia gates) and at least that many on the seaward side (St Paul, Arsenal, Arnaldus, Sea and St Catherine gates). The siege of 1480 seems to have demonstrated the vulnerability of gates in defence, as their number in the more vulnerable mainland sector was decreased in the ensuing modernization. Two of the five gates (St George and Acandia) were filled up, and formidable outworks were built in front of the remaining three.

Parapets, loopholes and machicolations

The 15th-century parapet of the fortress of Rhodes consisted of merlons and crenels. Today, rectangular merlons can only occasionally be seen on its walls and towers. However, according to the miniatures of Caoursin, an eyewitness of the siege of 1480, the whole of the fortress was provided with merlons at that time. More typical of the fortress of Rhodes today are merlons shaped like a swallowtail or a double swallowtail. The former may have appeared here in the early 16th century, when several North Italian craftsmen lived and worked on the island. In Italy merlons shaped like swallowtails signified that the owner of the castle belonged to the Ghibellines, the supporters of Holy Roman Emperors (the shape of the merlons is supposed to represent the wings

ABOVE LEFT Merlon of a three-horned shape, a form that was traditional for the Hospitallers. A cruciform loophole is in the centre of the merlon. Any kind of weapon – a bow, crossbow or hand firearm – could be used to shoot through this loophole. In the bottom right-hand corner, on the level of the wall-walk, there is a round aperture for a small cannon.

ABOVE RIGHT
A machicolation: an overhanging structure arranged on stone corbels on the battlement level, which enabled the defenders to attack the enemy at the foot of a wall. Machicolations can be seen on many towers of the sea wall of the Rhodes Fortress. After the siege of 1480 they were removed nearly everywhere on the most vulnerable mainland walls as they could easily be destroyed by artillery.

RIGHT A *bretèche* – a small balcony with machicolations – was designed to eliminate the dead ground in the bend of a fortress wall. Three-horned merlons were characteristic of Hospitaller fortifications in the 15th and 16th centuries, and can be seen on the balcony's sides.

of the eagle on the emperor's coat of arms). The Ghibellines were opposed by the Guelphs, who supported the papacy. The latter left traditional rectangular merlons on their castles. Opposition between the two groups arose in the 12th century under Frederick I Barbarossa, emperor of the Holy Roman Empire, who endeavoured to submit the whole of Italy to his rule. Starting in Florence, the strife between the Ghibellines and the Guelphs quickly spread all over Italy. By the 15th century swallow-tailed merlons were more typical of the castles of Northern Italy, being rare in the fortifications of other Italian regions, where ordinary rectangular merlons were preferred. Perhaps merlons shaped like a double swallowtail (three-horned) may be considered a sign of Hospitaller presence. Even four-horned merlons can occasionally be seen on Rhodes, and in some sectors the parapet is crowned with numerous small teeth, resembling sawteeth. All these forms of merlon take their root in the shape of a swallowtail – they arise when two or more merlons shaped like a swallowtail are placed next to each other, without crenels in between. All the forms of parapet – rectangular, swallowtail, double swallowtail and sawteeth – are to be seen in other castles built by the Order in that period.

On the inner sides of the merlons there are stone juts into which a crosspiece with a rotating crenel cover was fastened. The cover protected the defenders on the wall-walk from enemy fire. When shooting, defenders either raised the cover slightly or shot through a loophole in the cover.

The early 16th century saw changes in the parapets in the most vulnerable sections of the fortress of Rhodes. A thin battlemented parapet easily destroyed by artillery fire was replaced by a thick one of a rounded shape supplied with bell-shaped embrasures widening on the outside, specially designed for artillery. The changes affected the main wall and bulwarks in front of the towers on the mainland side. Low outworks, low outer walls and sea walls preserved their old battlemented parapet.

Machicolations, *bretèches* and plunging loopholes were commonplace in the old 15th-century walls of Rhodes. A machicolation was usually built on top of a tower and above a gate, and a *bretèche* (a small balcony with machicolations) over a gate and in the corners of the fortress wall. Plunging loopholes were placed in other, less crucial points where dead ground at the foot of a wall could not be covered by fire. In the early 16th century these overhanging structures shared the fate of the thin battlemented parapet;

ABOVE LEFT A mid-15th-century artillery loophole, viewed from the inside. These gun ports were designed for cannon manned by two people. One man put the barrel of the cannon into the lower aperture and aimed the cannon, following the directions of a gun aimer at the vision slit. The latter kept watch on the situation waiting for the proper moment and then fired a shot by igniting the primer with a slow-burning fuse.

ABOVE RIGHT This plunging loophole that allowed the defenders to command the foot of the wall (in the centre) is flanked by vertical slits with a triangular widening at the bottom. While the bottom widening allowed the enemy approaching the wall to be attacked, it did not provide for plunging fire. An *escutcheon* with the coats of arms of the Order of St John and Grand Master Pierre d'Aubusson can be seen on the left.

LEFT Parapet with four-horned merlons. Stone juts for fastening wooden rotating crenel covers were made on the edges of the merlons. There is an earlier gun port – a vertical slit above a round opening – in the centre of the merlon. An *escutcheon* with the coats of arms of the Order of St John and Grand Master Pierre d'Aubusson is in the bottom right-hand corner.

they were easily destroyed by artillery fire and so they too had to be given up. These changes concerned only the mainland side; the sea walls and internal fortifications remained as they were.

The walls of the Rhodian Fortress boast various shapes of loopholes for firing hand firearms: vertical slits, vertical slits with a triangular widening at the bottom, cruciform loopholes and vertical slits with a round opening at the bottom. The first and the second are believed to have been better suited for archers, the third to be suited for archers and crossbowmen and the fourth for hand firearms. This is, however, a question of preference. An arquebusier could certainly fire through a cruciform loophole and an archer could use a vertical slit with a round opening at the bottom. A crossbowman, whose weapon required a strictly horizontal opening, was hardest to place. Following the invention of the matchlock, hand firearms began ousting bows and crossbows from European armies in the late 15th and particularly early 16th centuries, yet it did not fully replace earlier ranged weapons at first. This accounts for the variety of loophole types. It cannot be said that common vertical slits, which seem the most archaic, were only characteristic of early defences. They can be easily seen both on sea walls and over d'Amboise Gate as well as in other, later sections of fortifications. In 1480 the crossbow remained the main long-range hand weapon; the bow and hand firearms were less popular. By 1522 hand firearms had replaced most other ranged weapons, but this only happened shortly before the siege so the older shapes of loophole remained.

Earlier artillery embrasures have a rectangular or round opening at the bottom for the gun barrel, and a vision slit at the top. Slits could be either vertical or horizontal with a round opening in the middle. These gun ports were designed for guns manned by two people. One manipulated the gun following the directions of the gun aimer at a vision slit, while the latter, watchful of the situation, waited for the proper moment to fire the gun by igniting the priming powder with a slow-burning fuse. Later artillery embrasures, those on the ground floor of Del Carretto Bulwark (1515–17) for instance, are of a completely different shape. This embrasure widens towards the outside and looks like a horizontal bay with an arched top.

Ditch

The ditch, which ran along the perimeter of the fortress on the landward side, was dry, following the principles of artillery fortification. Moreover, fortifications appeared as if they were embedded in the ditch – even the main wall, to say nothing of low outworks, were raised only slightly above the outer wall of the ditch (the counterscarp). Thus positioned, the defences were protected from artillery fire. Seen from the bottom of the ditch, however, the walls were as high as the walls of a medieval castle, and as difficult to escalade. In the course of modernization at the turn of the 15th and 16th centuries the ditch was considerably widened and in many places was divided into two parts by *tenailles*.

Its large width and depth excluded the possibility of it being filled in, and the ditch often became the arena of furious skirmishes. Finding themselves at its bottom the enemy were subject to both frontal and flanking fire. Heavy enfilade fire was brought to bear upon them from low outworks and projecting towers. For this purpose many bulwarks (St George Bastion, Del Carretto Bulwark and the bulwark in front of the Tower of Spain) were provided with embrasures at ground level.

Ditch at the Post of Provence. The Tower of Italy and the Del Carretto Bulwark are on the right. On the left, there is a stone-faced counterscarp. To climb down so high and almost vertical a slope is difficult even in peaceful circumstances, so to do so under enemy fire would be extremely dangerous.

Several posterns led from the fortress into the ditch to enable the defenders to make sallies and attack the enemy on the flanks. The posterns were small doorways usually on the ground floor near a bulwark or *tenaille*; there were also underground posterns with an exit in the middle of the ditch. The latter were probably disguised.

Outworks

Outworks of various shapes can be seen in the fortress walls of Rhodes. They can be divided into barbicans protecting gates, bulwarks protecting towers and *tenailles* protecting curtains and *caponiers*.

Of special interest for those studying the history of fortification are the bulwark-barbicans in front of the towers of St John and St George (there used to be gates there). They had an ideal pentagonal shape with an acute angle facing towards the direction of the enemy. These bulwarks could be considered true bastions but for the thinness of their front and flanking walls, which were unable to withstand strong artillery fire. They doubtless lacked the solidity acquired by 16th-century bastions, which had an earthen filling. Therefore, although supplied with gun ports, these bulwarks were more like barbicans

An underground postern leading into the ditch. Such sallyports offered an opportunity to unexpectedly attack the enemy in the ditch, and were probably disguised at the time of the sieges.

The Tower of Italy and the semicircular Del Carretto Bulwark in front of it, within the Post of the Italian langue. Built by Grand Master Fabrizio del Carretto in 1515–17, the bulwark is about 50m in diameter and has six embrasures and two sallyports at ground level. Thus this sector of the fortifications provided three tiers of cannon fire (two in the bulwark and one in the tower). Moreover, the cannon embrasures looked out in different directions, thus providing for frontal and flanking fire.

protecting the gate and tower behind them than genuine gun platforms. Nevertheless, these bulwark-barbicans were undoubtedly a step forwards in the development of the shape and structure of a true bastion. Unfortunately, we lack the exact dating of each structure. The bulwark at the Tower of St John was probably built under Grand Master Piero Raimundo Zacosta (1461–67) judging by his coat of arms on it. As to the bulwark at the Tower of St George, it was later absorbed into St George Bastion and the time of its construction is unclear. It may have been built together with the bulwark at the Tower of St John.

St George Bastion was certainly the most powerful stronghold in the fortress of Rhodes. Erected in 1496, it was of pentagonal form, though a little irregular. The bastion was an excellent gun platform. Its acute angle directed towards the enemy had extremely thick walls filled with earth. Its flanks had two-tier mural galleries with gun ports allowing flanking fire to be brought to bear upon the ditch. An underground countermine gallery began from the bastion and ran under the ditch. This bulwark became the first true pentagonal bastion, despite some imperfections. For instance, the two faces of the bastion could not be commanded from the adjacent fortifications. It should be remembered, however, that it was one of the first bastions in the world. Even in Italy the structure was just being developed at that time.

Arranged in chronological order of their appearance, the artillery bulwarks constructed in front of the towers of the Rhodian Fortress are: the bulwark of England (1487, irregular polygonal), the bulwark of Provence (before 1489, irregular polygonal), the bulwark of Spain (1489, slightly distorted pentagonal) and the bulwark of Auvergne (1496, almost ideally

B   FORTIFICATIONS OF THE POST OF ITALY READY TO FACE THE SIEGE OF 1522

The previous siege had revealed the weakness of the fortifications in this sector; on 27 June 1480 the Turks broke through the defences here and nearly captured the city. After the siege of 1480, the Hospitallers had the fortifications restored and strengthened with a solid earthwork (*tenaille*); they also had the semicircular Del Carretto Bulwark built in front of the Tower of Italy in 1515–17.

pentagonal). These ten years (from 1487 to 1496) witnessed steady advances towards the regularity and pentagonal form characteristic of a true bastion.

Later, however, engineers on Rhodes and those in Italy chose different ways to progress. The early 16th century saw the pentagonal bastion being further developed in Italy, while pentagonal bulwarks were abandoned in Rhodian fortifications in favour of semicircular ones, strongly resembling the fortifications of the so-called castles of Henry VIII in England. Del Carretto Bulwark in the Italian Post offers an excellent example of these semicircular bulwarks. Pentagonal forms would regain their dominance in the Order's fortifications after they settled on Malta.

Caponiers should not escape the attention of those interested in Rhodian fortifications. The honour of erecting these revolutionary structures (for their time) belongs to Grand Master Fabrizio del Carretto, as is proved by his coat of arms on the best-preserved *caponier* in the north-western corner of the fortress, near d'Amboise Gate. The date 1514 is indicated under the coat of arms. The *caponier* is a low, stretched one-storey building with a gable roof. Inside, the building is divided into four rooms, each supplied with two gun ports looking out on two different sides, so the *caponier* has four gun ports on each side. Positioned at the bottom of the ditch and placed well forwards towards the enemy, *caponiers* provided effective flanking fire leaving no dead ground.

TOUR OF THE FORTRESS

To appreciate the fortifications of the city of Rhodes as they deserve to be appreciated, it is best to examine them on the inside going along the wall-walk, and on the outside walking on the outer side of the ditch or along its bottom. It will certainly take twice as much time and effort, but you will be able to imagine yourself as a defender and a besieger in turn, not just an outsider studying the peculiarities of the fortifications. It will allow you to assess the weak and strong points of each sector of the defence.

A tour around the Rhodian fortifications is best started at Cannon Gate, which is near the Grand Masters' Palace. The gate itself is worth your attention: thoroughly restored, Cannon Gate is flanked with two round towers supplied with machicolations and crowned with swallowtail-shaped merlons. Having climbed up onto the wall-walk, you will find yourself above St Anthony Gate. A damaged relief of St Anthony has been preserved above the gate. In the north, one can see an outwork together with d'Amboise Gate; the polygonal Battery of the Olives with Pagnac Tower is visible in the distance. The complex of fortifications comprising Cannon Gate and St Anthony Gate, as well as the Battery of the Olives, was built under de Lastic (1437–54), and his coat of arms has been preserved on the walls of these fortifications. Later, at the time of d'Aubusson (1476–1503), the fortifications were strengthened on the outside with a thick earthen outwork. In 1512 d'Amboise built a gate here that was named after him (d'Amboise Gate). The gateway lies between two solid round squat towers. Beyond d'Amboise Gate, in the ditch, in the extreme north-west corner of the fortress, there is a *caponier* built by del Carretto in 1514. Grand masters were responsible for this sector during the first siege (1480), but by the time of the second siege (1522) the sector was divided between the langues of Germany and France with the border running through d'Amboise Gate.

D'Amboise Gate. A marble plaque over the gate tells us that the gate was built under Grand Master Emery d'Amboise in 1512. On the plaque, there is a relief of an angel holding the coat of arms of the Order and d'Amboise and the inscription 'DAMBOYSE MDXII (1512)'. Vertical slits above the gateway point to there having been a drawbridge in front of the gate.

Following the wall-walk along the mainland walls in a southerly direction, you will soon reach the German Post. It runs as far as St George Bastion, which belonged to the Auvergne Post. St George Bastion replaced earlier fortifications built here in 1421–31, as is witnessed by the coats of arms of Fluvian and Pope Martin V visible under the relief of St George on the western side of the tower. Those previous fortifications consisted of a rectangular tower and a gate, which was reached by a stone bridge. It was the main gate of the city at that time, leading straight to the marketplace. The pentagonal bulwark-barbican in front of the tower may have been built in the mid-15th century. In 1496 d'Aubusson blocked up the gate and built a powerful bastion of a slightly irregular shape opposite the tower. The bastion seems to have been built as a detached structure, and its flank reached no farther than the lower outer wall. It was only later, in 1521/22, that Grand Master de l'Isle Adam joined the flanks of the bastion and the curtains of the main wall, incarnating in stone the drawings of the Italian engineer Basilio dalla Scuola di Vicenza. Restoring the parapet on the bastion after the siege of 1522, the Turks made a mistake, so that today it does not look the same as it did during the siege. At that time the bastion had a formidable artillery parapet as had the rest of the bulwarks.

The next interesting place is the Tower of Spain. By the decree issued by Zacosta in 1465 the tower belonged to the Post of England that extended from here to the Tower of the Virgin Mary. During the siege of 1480 the English knights defended the sector. Later, however, the posts of the English and Aragon langues switched their sectors of defence and in 1522 it was the Spanish knights who defended the sector. Since that time the tower has been called the Tower of Spain. It is a round tower projecting prominently beyond the line of the walls, and used to be joined to them by short cross-walls. It is 3m higher than the adjoining curtains. In 1489 a bulwark of a slightly distorted pentagonal shape was built in front of the tower. Both the Spanish and English posts (for convenience, we shall refer to them according to their later positions, where they were in the siege of 1522) were provided with powerful advanced earthworks (*tenailles*) built in the ditch, in front of the main walls.

The Spanish Post was originally (when it still was English) constructed in such a way that the two walls between the jutting towers formed a corner open towards the enemy. It was a wise layout. Even as far back as the

Fortifications of the posts of Germany and France in 1522

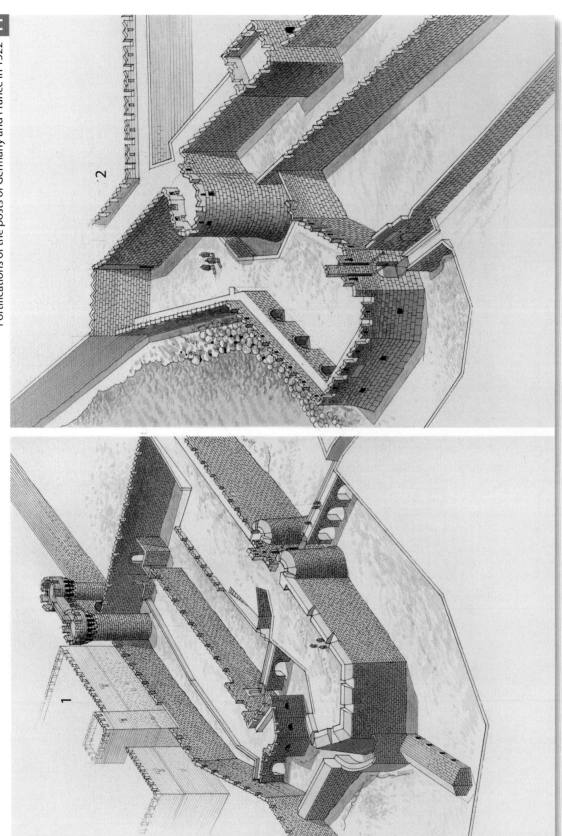

3rd century BC Philon of Byzantium recommended building curtains in this way. The enemy wishing to attack the curtain found themselves in an extremely disadvantageous position, under crossfire from the convergent walls as well as the towers. In addition, there was a lower outer wall strengthened with two rectangular towers and a jog set in front of the formidable inner wall. Coats of arms show that the earlier defences consisting of a double wall were erected at the time of Fluvian (1421–37). Orsini (1467–76) had the ditch widened. Finally, probably under del Carretto (1513–21), an embankment was made to thicken the main wall and a parapet with embrasures for cannon was added.

The Post of Spain reaches as far as the Tower of the Virgin Mary, which belonged to the English Post. The Tower of the Virgin Mary was erected in 1441/42 by de Lastic (his coat of arms can be seen under the relief of the Virgin Mary and Child). At the time of the erection of the tower the post belonged to the langue of Aragon. Probably because of that the tower was built in the Spanish–Portuguese 'albarra' style (i.e. it was a free-standing structure). Later, Orsini had it joined to the wall with short cross-walls, and d'Aubusson built a large polygonal bulwark in front of the tower.

Neighbouring the Tower of the Virgin Mary is St Athanassios Gate. The gate is complex, protected with several defensive elements. To enter the fortress one has first to get across a polygonal outwork protecting the tower, then cross a drawbridge leading to the wall-walk of the outer wall and

View of the Spanish (originally English) Post. Seen in the foreground is an earthwork (*tenaille*) faced with stone; in the distance is the Tower of Spain with its bulwark. Note how gun ports on the ground level of the bulwark command the ditch.

C FORTIFICATIONS OF THE POSTS OF GERMANY AND FRANCE IN 1522

This is a reconstruction of how the defences at d'Amboise Gate **(1)** and the Gate of St Paul **(2)** would have looked in 1522. The construction of the complex of fortifications near the Grand Masters' Palace was begun under Jean de Lastic (1437–54), who also built the Cannon and St Anthony gates, as well as the Battery of the Olives. Pierre d'Aubusson (1476–1503) had it strengthened with a thick earthen outwork, which was cut through with a gate (d'Amboise Gate) under Emery d'Amboise in 1512. In 1514 Grand Master Fabrizio del Carretto had a *caponier* built in the ditch on the extreme north-west corner of the fortress, beyond d'Amboise Gate. The Gate of St Paul was protected on the outside with a polygonal barbican. Although the walls of the barbican were adjusted to accommodate artillery, they were fairly thin and crowned with a merloned parapet. The fortifications have been preserved nearly unchanged since the mid-15th century. There are no solid earthen bulwarks, wide ditches, thick walls or artillery parapets characteristic of the fortifications of the late 15th and early 16th centuries among them.

The English Post viewed from the Tower of the Virgin Mary. The post initially belonged to the langue of Aragon in accordance with the decree of 1465, and in 1480 was defended by Spanish knights. Later, however, the posts of the English and Aragon langues changed places and in the siege of 1522 this sector was defended by the English. On the left, near a rectangular tower, St Athanassios Gate is visible.

go on along the main wall to find oneself in front of the high rectangular Tower of St Athanassios. Like other towers of this sector, the Tower of St Athanassios was a free-standing structure connected to the wall by small bridges. It was provided with machicolations on at least three sides. The gateway lay between the tower and the main wall. The tower was later joined to the wall so the gateway is now inside the tower. The Tower of St Athanassios is adorned with a relief of the Church Father and the coat of arms of Fluvian beneath it. Above the gate arch on the side of the city there is the coat of arms of del Carretto (1513–21) in the claws of an eagle. Del Carretto seems to have been responsible for the thickening of the main wall from the inside. It was, however, d'Aubusson who had the polygonal bulwark built and the Gate of St Athanassios finished in 1487. A small marble plate discovered in the wall confirms this. The plate carries an inscription and the coat of arms of d'Aubusson and was re-used as building material by the Turks in 1530/31 in the course of the restoration of this sector, which was seriously damaged in the siege of 1522.

The Post of England strongly resembles that of Spain. The wall between the projecting towers also bends a little here, a lower wall with four rectangular towers sits in front of the main wall, and there is a thick earthen *tenaille* running in the middle of the ditch in front of the curtain.

On passing along the Post of England we find ourselves at the Gate of St John. It is also known as Koskinou Gate or the Red Door. A marble tablet on the wall carries a bilingual inscription, in Italian and Greek, informing us that the construction of this sector was finished in 1457 under

D FORTIFICATIONS OF THE ARAGON POST (1480), LATER THE ENGLISH POST (1522)

During the siege of 1480 this sector belonged to the langue of Aragon but later the posts of England and Aragon changed places, and in the siege of 1522 the sector was defended by English knights. In 1480 (1) the defences of the sector comprised a double wall fortified by several towers, the strongest of which is the Tower of the Virgin Mary situated at the corner of a fortress wall. St Athanassios Gate is next to the tower, and the road to the gate lay by a small drawbridge near the Tower of the Virgin Mary, then along the wall-walk of the outer wall and to the gate in the rectangular Tower of St Athanassios. By 1487 Grand Master Pierre d'Aubusson had the ditch considerably widened, a large polygonal bulwark built in front of the Tower of the Virgin Mary and a thick earthen *tenaille* made in the middle of the ditch, in front of the rest of the walls of the sector. That is what the English Post looked like when it was challenged with the siege of 1522 (2).

1

2

the supervision of the Greek master mason Manolis Kountis. In fact, this sector began to be fortified earlier, under Fluvian (1421–37). Erected at this time was the rectangular Tower of St John and his coat of arms can be seen on the tower, a little below the relief of St John the Baptist. The ground floor of the tower originally housed a church, but was later filled in with stones to increase its defensive capability. Thanks to Italian restorers, the ground floor is clear of stones now. A pentagonal bulwark-barbican that embraced the tower was built later, probably under Zacosta (1461–67), which is asserted by this grand master's coat of arms over the gate. The bulwark-barbican was crowned with a battlemented parapet with slits and rectangular loopholes for cannon and had a gate in the flank. Between 1481 and 1489, in front of the tower with the bulwark-barbican a large, irregular-shaped bulwark was built, connected with the opposite side of the ditch by a stationary bridge that ended with a drawbridge at the gate. D'Aubusson's coat of arms can be seen in four places on these fortifications.

The defences by the Gate of St John belonged to the Post of Provence and extended as far as the Tower of Italy. The walls of this sector had a zigzag trace and were fortified with three projecting towers: a triangular one with a bulwark of the same shape, a round one having a polygonal bulwark and a rectangular tower with a rectangular bulwark. The position of the coats of arms shows that the fortifications were created at the time of de Milly and d'Aubusson, while the main wall was thickened under del Carretto.

The Post of Provence is followed by the Italian Post, its chief fortifications being the Tower of Italy and the Del Carretto Bulwark. There used to be the Acandia Gate here, but it was blocked up around 1480. The tower is a round squat structure topped with cannon embrasures instead of a battlemented parapet. A semicircular bulwark with embrasures of the same shape protects the tower on the outside. Built under del Carretto in 1515–17, the bulwark is about 50m in diameter and has six embrasures on ground level with two sallyports. Thus, the sector provided three tiers of gunfire (two in the bulwark and one in the tower) with the gun embrasures looking out on different sides providing both frontal and flanking fire.

The Italian Post ends at St Catherine Gate. The siege of 1480 revealed the weakness of this sector: on 27 June the Turks broke through the defence line here and nearly captured the city. Therefore, right after the siege the Hospitallers restored and strengthened the fortifications. By 1489 solid earthen outworks had been built here.

St Catherine Gate was set at an angle, and was supplied with a portcullis and machicolations over the gateway. It is one of the gates leading to the harbour. More famous is the Sea Gate, situated in the centre of the bay. The Sea Gate is flanked by two powerful round towers with a battlemented parapet and machicolations. The large relief over the gate depicts the Virgin Mary, St John the Baptist, St Paul and the coats of arms of the Order of St John, France and d'Aubusson. It carries

The Sea Gate. It is the major gate connecting the city with the Commercial Harbour. Above the gateway there is large relief depicting the Virgin Mary, St John the Baptist and St Paul. It is adorned with the coats of arms of the Order of St John, France and Grand Master Pierre d'Aubusson, and carries the date 1478, the year when the gate was either built or modernized.

the date 1478. It is unclear, though, whether the gate was built in that year or merely modernized.

Moving along the bay to the north you will reach Arsenal Gate (also known as Dockyard or Tarsana Gate). Its gateway is unusually wide and high – 9.9m and 5m respectively. The size of the gate can be explained only by the necessity of pulling vessels through it. The shipbuilding yard was inside the fortifications until at least 1480.

The wall along the harbour is not as strong as the mainland one. It is thinner (only 2.1m thick) and has a battlemented parapet instead of one with gun embrasures. A lower outer wall once running at the foot of the seawall does not survive. By a decree of 1465, the responsibility for the defence of the seawall was divided between the langues of France (the northern part of the walls) and Castile (their southern part). By the time of the siege of 1522, however, the whole sector of fortifications alongside the harbour was assigned to the Post of Castile.

The northern part of Rhodian fortifications was under the authority of the French langue. A zigzag wall running from the sea to the Grand Masters' Palace was strengthened with two round and three rectangular towers. Between the round towers (St Peter and St Paul towers) are the two oldest surviving towers built by the Hospitallers. They date from 1377–96. Just by the sea, protected by the Tower of St Paul or Trebuc Tower is St Paul Gate with a barbican of a complex polygonal shape in front of it, which is reached by drawbridge. Although the walls of the barbican could accommodate

Arsenal Gate. The gate has an unusually wide (9.9m) and high (5m) passage, which was due to the need to tug vessels through it, as the ship-building yard was (at least before 1480) inside the defences. The Grand Masters' Palace can be seen in the background.

E **FOLLOWING PAGE: FORTIFICATIONS OF THE POST OF PROVENCE IN 1480 AND 1522**

The fortifications of the Post of Provence were considerably enhanced between 1480 (1) and 1522 (2). The fortifications have a zigzag trace and are strengthened with three projecting towers: triangular, round and rectangular, each protected by a bulwark. The Tower and Bulwark of St John is the chief stronghold. The rectangular Tower of St John was erected under Grand Master Antonio Fluvian (1421–37), while Piero Raimundo Zacosta (1461–67) built a pentagonal bulwark-barbican in front of it. The bulwark-barbican, the flank of which was provided with a gate, was identical to that set in front of St George Tower, and a step forwards on the way to a new shape and structure of a true bastion. Between the years 1481 and 1489 a large irregular bulwark was built in front of these fortifications, connected with the opposite side of the ditch by a stone bridge that led to a small drawbridge at the gate.

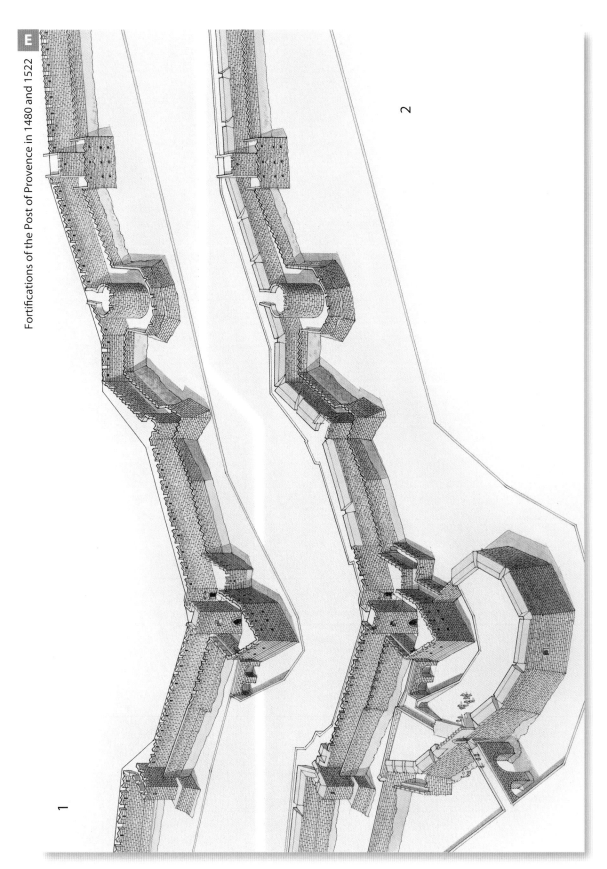

1

2

Towers and forts that protected the entrance to the harbours of the city of Rhodes in the early 16th century: Fort St Nicholas **(1)**, the Naillac Tower **(2)** and the Tower of the Windmills **(3)**. At first the extremities of all the three Rhodian moles acquired a free-standing tower each: St Nicholas Tower (1464–67) was built on the far northern mole, the Naillac Tower (1396–1421) on the nearer short northern mole and the Tower of the Windmills (1440–54) on the eastern mole. After the siege of 1480 Grand Master Pierre d'Aubusson (1476–1503) reconstructed and made into forts St Nicholas Tower and the Tower of the Windmills. The earthquake of 1863 destroyed the Naillac Tower and here it is reconstructed after its image in the miniatures of Caoursin.

artillery, they are too thin and are topped with a battlemented parapet. On the whole, the defences of the sector are typical of the mid-15th century. There are no solid earthen bulwarks, nor broad ditches, thick walls or artillery parapets so characteristic of the late 15th and early 16th centuries. Thus we can conclude that these fortifications were most likely built at the time of Zacosta (1461–67). In 1477 (under d'Aubusson, whose coat of arms can also be seen here) the thickness of the main wall was increased to 5.2m.

The eastern and northern sides of the commercial harbour were enclosed with moles. The Hospitallers constructed towers on their extremities: the Tower of the Windmills on the eastern mole and the Naillac Tower on the northern. The eastern mole projected 300m into the sea and was covered with windmills in the middle ages (hence the name of the tower). The Hospitallers had about 15 mills here, but under the Turks the number was reduced to three. Built in 1440–54 on the very tip of the mole, the Tower

Barbican by St Paul Gate, viewed from both the outside and inside. The walls of the barbican were adjusted to accommodate artillery (with gun ports at ground level). They are too thin, however, to withstand an extended bombardment and are crowned with a battlemented parapet with three-horned merlons, which are characteristic of Hospitaller fortifications. These features are typical of fortifications dating from around the mid-15th century, so the defences seem to have been erected at the time of Grand Master Piero Raimundo Zacosta (1461–67).

Fort St Nicholas. Originally built as a round tower in 1464–67, it was encircled with an outwork and turned into a fort after the siege of 1480. Situated on the tip of an ancient mole, this outpost protects the entrance to Mandraki harbour and the northern approaches to the fortress. Because of its strategic position it was frequently a target of violent attacks, particularly during the siege of 1480.

of the Windmills looked different from how it does today. In the centre of the 12m-diameter tower rose a polygonal turret. The tower could be entered from the first floor by a drawbridge that connected it with a tiny staircase-turret standing 2m away. Inside the turret there was a spiral staircase leading up from the ground floor. The Tower of the Windmills was seriously damaged during the siege of 1480 and changed considerably in the course of the restoration under d'Aubusson – it was deprived of the polygonal turret on top but acquired an outwork.

The Naillac Tower on the extremity of the northern mole was built under de Naillac (1396–1421) and named after him. It was a rectangular tower 37m in height and had four round turret-bartizans on the top of each side. It was crowned with a 9m-high octagonal turret in the centre, which had a spiral staircase on the inside leading to its top. With its total height reaching 46m the Naillac Tower served as an excellent watchtower and lighthouse. Unfortunately, the earthquake of 1863 did not spare it and today we can see only its basement. A chain thrown across the port had one end fastened to the Tower of the Windmills and the other to the Naillac Tower.

The isolated Fort St Nicholas built on the extremity of an ancient mole protects the entrance to Mandraki harbour and the northern approaches to the fortress. At first Zacosta had a round tower 17.3m in diameter, built there in 1464–67. Called St Nicholas Tower, it was adorned with a relief of St Nicholas and the coats of arms of Zacosta and the Duke of Burgundy, who financed its construction. Like the Tower of the Windmills, St Nicholas Tower was entered through a detached staircase-turret. Gravely damaged in the siege of 1480 and the earthquake of 1481 the tower was restored and encircled with a solid outwork by d'Aubusson, who turned it into a powerful fort. The staircase-turret was amalgamated into the core structure and a small chapel dedicated to St Nicholas was built inside the thick walls. Owing to its advantageous strategic position the tower, and then the fort, were subject to violent attacks in the course of both Turkish sieges; even during World War II the fort was adapted to fit guns and machine guns.

Besides fortifications erected in Rhodes by the Order of St John, the city has preserved some remains of Byzantine defences, which the Hospitallers used as an inner wall separating the knights' residences from the rest of the city, populated by Greeks. The first Byzantine wall was built as far back as the 7th century; the second one rose parallel to the first and was 10–12m

Ruins of the inner wall of the fortress of Rhodes that separated the knights' quarters (Collachium) from the southern part of the city (Chora or Bourga). The wall had been built by the Byzantines, and the Hospitallers merely maintained it.

further south in the late 11th or early 12th century. The walls survive in places in a section extending about 500m from the Guardia Tower, later turned into the Clock Tower, on the west of the wall built by the Hospitallers along the harbour. The wall runs roughly along Theofiliskou and Agisandrou streets. Its eight surviving towers are in different stages of preservation. The easternmost tower was repaired at the time of de Heredia (1376–96), which is witnessed by his coat of arms on the tower. The knights turned the inside of the tower into a church. In 1475 the Hospitallers dug out a deep and wide ditch in front of the Byzantine wall and built outworks in front of the gates and some of the towers.

Windmills were characteristic of medieval Rhodes. They could be seen all around the city and on both harbour moles. The windmills were circular tower-like structures with a movable timber roof. Most of them were used to grind wheat, but some were also used for grinding powder. Some of the windmills are still there.

One of the windmills preserved outside the city walls of Rhodes. This tower-like structure was once covered with a timber roof. A windmill grinding wheat and gunpowder was a typical feature of Rhodes.

THE LIVING SITES

An inner wall divided the city of Rhodes into two parts: the northern part, known as Collachium, and the southern, known as Chora or Bourga. The smaller in size, Collachium housed the main administrative and residential buildings of the Order of St John: the Grand Masters' Palace, the Hospital, the main churches, the Knights' apartments, inns and so on. The local population, mostly Greek, inhabited the larger southern part. The inner defensive wall attested to the Knights' lack of confidence in the local population and their intention to secure themselves against possible insurrections.

Grand Masters' Palace

The Grand Masters' Palace, a high, rectangular structure with towers and battlemented parapets, dominates the north-western corner of the fortress. Fortified and attached to the fortress walls, the palace was part of the city's defence system, and at the same time it was a citadel, the last resort of the Knights of St John in case the city was lost.

The palace had replaced a Byzantine citadel built on this site in the 7th century. As soon as they arrived on the island, the Hospitallers set about reconstructing the old fortress and erecting the Grand Masters' Palace in its place. The coat of arms of Grand Master Hélion de Villeneuve (1319–46) that can be seen above the south gate of the palace confirms the first half of the 14th century as the time the work was started.

The foundation of a formidable rectangular tower near the northwest corner of the palace has been preserved from the Byzantine fortress. The Knights made an earthen rampart in front of the tower to accommodate a battery of guns here.

The palace was not just the Grand Masters' apartments, it was the administrative centre of the entire Order of St John. It had two entrances – one on the southern side, the other on the western side. The southern gate was the main gate. It was flanked by two powerful U-shaped towers at the gate. The western gate was protected by a high rectangular tower, probably built in the late 15th century in the course of restoration works after either the Turkish siege of 1480 or the earthquake of 1481.

In 1856 the upper part of the palace fell down. What we can see today is the reconstruction carried out by the Italian

View of the Post of Germany. The squat d'Amboise Gate can be seen in the distance. On the right the Grand Masters' Palace towers over the walls. The ditch is at its widest here.

government in 1937–40. However, the primary object of the reconstruction was the creation of a magnificent palace rather than the restoration of the historical image of the building. Under the Knights of St John the walls and towers were crowned differently, and the interior of the rooms of the upper floor were also different. At the time of the Hospitallers the ceilings of the halls and residential quarters were most likely made of timber and decorated with pictures of geometrical and floral design, as well as animals and human figures. Stained-glass windows depicted the figures of saints, the Grand Masters' coats of arms and other designs.

There was a courtyard in the centre of the palace, where ten huge silos for storing grain had once been dug into the ground. Three of them that were later shaped into marble well heads can still be seen in the eastern corner of the yard.

The living quarters and offices in the palace consisted of a number of rooms built around the courtyard. The ground floor was occupied by magazines, stables, kitchens and other auxiliary services. The upper floors housed the 'Great Hall' or 'Great Council Chamber', the banqueting hall, the Grand Master's apartments and other living quarters or a place of general assemblage.

Today the palace accommodates a museum displaying Hellenistic, Roman and early Byzantine statues and mosaics mainly from Kos, along with 16th-century Western European furniture.

Hospital

Settled on Rhodes, the Order of St John continued to see to one of its main missions in tending the sick, the poor and orphaned children as well as giving help to pilgrims on the way to the Holy Land. To fulfil this task the Knights built a hospital in Rhodes. Judging by the surviving inscriptions, the hospital that can be seen there today was built in 1440–89.

From an architectural point of view the hospital resembles eastern caravanserais or inns: a central rectangular courtyard surrounded by a two-storey gallery. Beyond the arched gallery there are rooms for various purposes (living quarters, storerooms, stables, kitchen, refectory and others). The distinctive feature of the hospital is, however, a long large hall on the eastern side of the building where the patients were accommodated. Similar halls are characteristic of Western European hospitals; they are not to be met with in eastern caravanserais.

Responsibility for maintaining the hospital and helping its patients rested upon the Grand Hospitaller, who was chosen from the langue of France. Subordinate to him was the *infermarius* elected once every two years, usually also from among the French. The position of *infermarius* was very important and the appointment was to be approved by the Grand Master and the council, to whom the candidate was introduced by the Grand Hospitaller. The *infermarius* was to visit the sick in the daytime and at night. Two advisors monitored his job. Moreover, each langue of the Order nominated a brother to supervise the tending of the sick. Accompanied by a scribe, these representatives of the langues were to see the sick twice a day to ensure the fulfilment of the doctors' instructions. The doctors were to examine the sick in the presence of the *infermarius* and eight brothers.

Anyone in need of care could become a patient of the hospital, but he had to say a confession, take Holy Communion and make his will. Patients were forbidden to play cards and dice or read books that were not connected with the Christian religion. They were to follow all the doctor's prescriptions and keep to a prescribed diet. In return they received a bed curtained on all sides and the most qualified medical treatment available at that time. It is characteristic that food was served to them on a silver tray.

The hospital building is fairly well preserved and carefully restored. There are even original wooden doors and roof timbers carrying the coats of arms of Grand Masters in some apartments. Today it houses an archaeological museum where ancient sculptures, reliefs, mosaics and vases are displayed.

The Street of the Knights, the inns and other old buildings

The Knights of St John had their own houses in the northern part of the city (Collachium), in the street known today as the Street of the Knights (Odos Ippoton). Being soldier-monks, the Knights spent much time in prayer and military exercises.

Every langue had its own inn in the Street of the Knights. Judging by descriptions, one can conclude that the inns were used for the meetings of the members of a langue, a kind of club. The knights could meet each other there, have dinner together and discuss their daily problems. They did not live in the inns, but noble travellers, pilgrims or refugees could stay there. These guests were usually settled according to their nationality, with the French staying at the inn of the langue of France and so on.

The inns were usually large buildings with a number of subsidiary rooms; they sometimes included gardens. All the inns had a horse-driven mill for drawing water. The interior of almost every inn comprised storerooms and a banqueting or assembly hall. Above the entrance to an inn one could see a coat of arms either of the royal house of the country, or of the Grand Master under whom the construction of the building began, or of some famous knights of the langue.

The size of an inn depended on the number of the brother-knights of the langue. The inns of Spain (for all the knights coming from the Iberian Peninsula) and France were the largest, then came the inns of Provence, Auvergne and Italy. The inns of England and Germany were the smallest. Except for the inn of Germany, all the inns of the above-mentioned langues survive. However, not all of them have been preserved intact as they were at the time of their construction (the 15th and early 16th century); some were restored, others partly destroyed.

The Street of the Knights (Odos Ippoton). About 200m long and about 6m wide, the street is flanked by the houses of the knights and the inns of the langues built some 500 years ago (late 15th to early 16th centuries). The inn of the langue of France, easily recognizable from its battlemented parapet with small turrets, can be seen on the opposite side of the street.

In the north-east corner of the Collachium, near the harbour, were the arsenal, the gunpowder store and the naval dockyard. No wonder it was there, at the end of the Street of the Knights, that the inns of the langues of Auvergne and Italy were, whose leaders were the Grand Marshal and the Admiral respectively. Only one of the large magazines of the arsenal survives. This site is supposed to have first been occupied by the hospital of the Order of St John. Later, however, in the 15th century, a new hospital was built, and the old one converted into an arsenal. The rectangular building with a single window near the top and a few ventilation apertures is today identified as the gunpowder store. The Knights of Rhodes left some more buildings, the designation of which is still to be guessed.

THE FORTRESS AT WAR

The Order of St John settled at Rhodes in 1309 and as early as 1310–12 and 1318/19 the Turks made weak and unsuccessful attempts to drive the knights from the island. Having risen to the challenge, the Hospitallers were awarded with 100 years of comparative peace. This does not mean that they ever really rested from wartime activity however. During the 14th and 15th centuries they were actively engaged in both sea and land battles. They harassed Turkish and Egyptian ships in the Aegean Sea, fought against the Turks for Morea (Peloponnesus), and even built and held several fortresses in Turkish Anatolia.

In 1440 the Egyptian Sultan tried to capture Rhodes. The Hospitallers attacked the landing enemy and finally destroyed the Egyptians in a bloody day-long naval battle. Unabated, the Egyptians made another attempt on Rhodes in 1444. The city was subjected to a 40-day siege and numerous attacks, all of which were beaten off. The Egyptians had to retreat empty handed.

In 1453 Sultan Mehmed II besieged and took Constantinople. This Turkish victory left the Order of St John based on Rhodes and some other offshore Anatolian islands the only Christian outpost close to the centre of the Ottoman Empire. The Order's aggressive naval policy undermined Turkish shipping and the delivery of goods to various parts of the empire. War between the Order and the Ottoman Empire was inevitable. 1480 marked the first Turkish attempt to put an end to the Hospitallers.

View of the Post of France. On the left is the Tower of St Paul. On the right is the barbican at St Paul Gate. The two oldest towers built by the Knights of St John (dating from 1377–96) can be seen in the distance.

The fortress of Rhodes in 1480

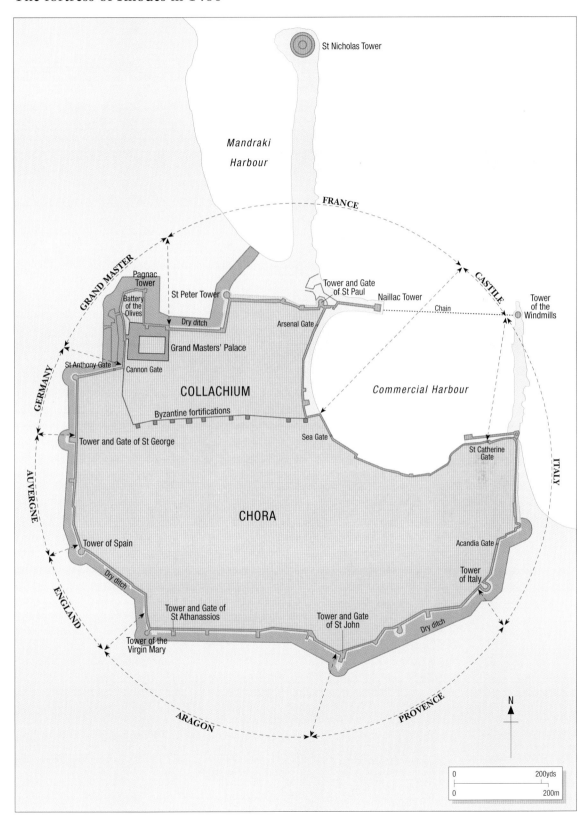

St Nicholas Tower

Mandraki Harbour

FRANCE

GRAND MASTER

Pagnac Tower

St Peter Tower

Battery of the Olives

Dry ditch

Tower and Gate of St Paul

Naillac Tower

CASTILE

Tower of the Windmills

Chain

Arsenal Gate

St Anthony Gate

Cannon Gate

Grand Masters' Palace

COLLACHIUM

GERMANY

Byzantine fortifications

Sea Gate

Commercial Harbour

Tower and Gate of St George

St Catherine Gate

AUVERGNE

ITALY

CHORA

Tower of Spain

Acandia Gate

Tower of Italy

Dry ditch

ENGLAND

Tower and Gate of St Athanassios

Tower and Gate of St John

Dry ditch

Tower of the Virgin Mary

ARAGON

PROVENCE

N

0   200yds
0   200m

1480

We will sooner die here than retreat.

What is more glorious than to die for the Faith?

Grand Master Pierre d'Aubusson
(during the siege of Rhodes in 1480)

The campaign was launched in the winter of 1479 with an intelligence operation headed by Misac Palaeologos Pasha, who supposedly came from the house of Palaeologos, and was appointed Vizier and Commander-in-Chief. Misac Pasha's fleet reached a remote point on the island of Rhodes where the Turks landed their troops, including the Sipahis, an elite mounted force (analogous to European knights). They began burning villages and ravaging the countryside. The local population sought shelter in castles while the Hospitallers dispersed the enemy and made them retreat.

Misac's army spent the rest of the winter at Physcos (Marmarice), on the Asia Minor coast opposite Rhodes. By April 1480 the main forces had arrived from Constantinople – the troops were delivered by land, and the siege artillery and heavy stores by sea. Contemporary chroniclers assert that the Turkish army was 100,000 men strong. However, available sources of information being solely European, it is quite possible that the figures were overestimated. Considering he needed troops for other campaigns, Mehmed II could hardly have detached more than 20,000 men to besiege Rhodes.

On the threshold of the siege all the inhabitants together with their cattle and poultry were evacuated to the city of Rhodes and other castles. The city was provided with a two-year supply of food, gunpowder and ammunition. The Augustinian monk Father de Curti wrote that 'The City is well provided with grain, wine, oil, cheese, salted meat and other foodstuffs … many crossbows and both heavy and light guns and earthenware fire-pots and receptacles for boiling oil and Greek fire and pots full of pitch lashed together … and there is a continuous watch by day and night of select companies of crossbowmen and hand-gunners and 100 cavalry' (Brockman, p.65).

The Hospitallers were well prepared for defence, as is clear from the extract. The strength of the garrison left much to be desired though; the Order's constant shortage of manpower now told on it. By modern calculations, the Rhodian garrison was no more than 2,500 men strong with 600 warrior-monks (knights and sergeants-at-arms) at most. All the rest were mercenaries or local militia. Thus, the Turkish army was at least eight times larger.

Turkish siege cannon of the period of the rule of Mehmed II the Conqueror (1451–81). The length of the bronze barrel is 4.24m, it weighs 15 tons and the calibre is 63cm. The walls of the barrel are 14cm thick. The projectile chamber is 1.86m long, the gunpowder chamber 1.67m long and the diameter of the gunpowder chamber is 23cm. The ball weighs 285kg.

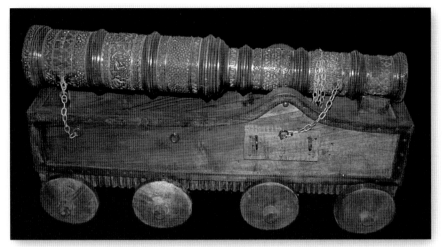

Wooden model of a Turkish siege cannon on a wheeled platform. The barrel of the cannon was fixed to the platform with the help of chains driven through special rings on the sides of the barrel. Such rings can be seen on many Turkish cannon of the 15th century. Carts like this were used to transport the barrel, but when it came to be fired, the barrel was put into a specially made wooden box or an earthen embankment.

On 23 May 1480, the lookout post on Mount St Stephen signalled that the Turkish armada was approaching Rhodes. That same evening, the Turks had already cast anchor in the Bay of Trianda and begun disembarking. The next day the city was surrounded by Turkish troops and siege artillery protected by gabions and abattis. The Turkish siege artillery included 16 huge bombards and a great number of mortars and cannon of smaller calibre.

Before firing his first shot Misac Pasha sent a herald to the city inviting the Knights to surrender and promising general amnesty and special privileges for the Greeks. The offer was rejected with scorn. Then the Turks began bombarding the city on all sides. Their targets were not only the fortifications, but living quarters as well – the enemy wished to shatter the morale of the Greek population and force it to yield. They also used fireballs and incendiary arrows to set fire to the city. D'Aubusson responded to this tactic with the organization of brigades specializing in putting out fires and arranging special shelters for the old, the feeble and children. As a result, the defenders' losses to the bombardment were insignificant.

The Turks made the St Nicholas Tower their chief target from the start. Having destroyed the tower, the Turks could bring their fleet into Mandraki harbour to support their attack on the northern walls of the city. So they positioned, opposite St Nicholas Tower, a special battery consisting of three enormous bronze bombards.

The tower withstood the bombardment for a long time. The bombards could fire no more than 14 shots a day, as the cooling and reloading of a big cannon of that epoch required a lot of time. The tower was solidly built and began to fall down only after 300 hits. During the bombardments the defenders never stopped communicating with the tower along the mole. Meanwhile, the Turks found themselves under constant fire from the city walls and sharpshooters positioned all along the mole.

Turkish cannon balls broke enormous lumps of stone fastened by mortar off the St Nicholas Tower. Nevertheless the defenders under the command of Fabrizio del Carretto, future Grand Master, managed to make an impregnable stronghold of the wreckage of the tower. Hundreds of workers – slaves, soldiers, sailors and women – were busy day and night turning the ruins into defences. Disregarding considerable losses in their ranks they dug out a ditch, constructed a palisade and drove stakes into the seabed in shallow waters on the approaches to the tower.

After ten days of bombardment the St Nicholas Tower was stormed for the first time. The Turks had re-equipped several galleys by strengthening their sides, making platforms on their bows and removing their masts, sails and all unnecessary rigging. These 'assault galleys' accommodated several cannon, and packed with soldiers they moved towards St Nicholas Tower. Their approach was accompanied by an unbearable noise with which the Turks hoped to frighten the defenders into panic. The galleys thundered with the sounds of pipes, cymbals, drums and eldritch screams. The defenders met the enemy with fire from crossbows, longbows and arquebuses, as well as fire-pots and Greek fire. At the same time, the galleys were an excellent target for the cannon on the walls of the French Post. One galley caught fire and sank. The others came close to the tower and started landing a party. The Turks jumped into the shallow waters and some of them fell upon stakes and were drowned. Many, however, managed to get to the shore where they engaged in furious hand-to-hand fighting with the knights. Fierce though the Turkish attack was, the knights fought bravely with

This miniature from the manuscript of Caoursin shows either the preparation for or the aftermath of an attack on St Nicholas Tower during the siege of 1480. A half-ruined St Nicholas Tower is in the foreground. A pontoon bridge leads to it from the opposite shore of the bay. The Turks crowded on the shore seem to be preparing to get across. However, the bridge is already broken in the middle and the Order's ships dominate the sea. The artist may have combined the events that happened before and after the assault in one miniature. (MS lat. 6067, fol. 80v, Bibliothèque nationale de France)

their great swords, and supported by crossbowmen, archers and hand-gunners they drove the enemy into the sea. The surviving Turks left in their galleys.

Two more attempts to seize St Nicholas Tower in the same way also failed. The last of them was undertaken on 9 June and ostensibly cost the Turks 600 men killed and as many wounded while the defenders did not lose a single man. Figures cited in Christian chronicles ought not, however, to be understood literally. The number '600' may possibly be interpreted as 'very many' and no losses among the defenders may refer only to the losses among the knights, as losses among common soldiers were not usually taken note of at that time.

On 7 June Misac Pasha positioned a battery of eight large bombards opposite the Italian Post. Another bombard was aimed at the Tower of the Windmills on the extremity of the eastern mole. Numerous mortars showered incendiaries on the densely populated Jewish Quarter situated beyond the fortifications of the Italian Post. The Turks decided to assault two sectors simultaneously – one to the south and the other to the north – thus forcing the defenders to split what little force they had.

Fortifications of the Italian Post soon began to yield and d'Aubusson realized that the time was not far off when the Turks would succeed in making a breach here. He ordered all the buildings in the Jewish Quarter pulled down and a semicircular retrenchment constructed beyond the fortifications of the Italian Post. Day and night, all citizens – knights, slaves, women, children and monks – dug out a ditch and piled up a rampart, topping it with a wall. At the same time the defenders tried to restore the breaches in the *enceinte*. The ground between the *enceinte* and retrenchment was riddled with trap-pits covered with branches and soil. Various types of weapons were accumulated on top of the rampart to be used against the enemy: kegs with tar and sulphur, Greek fire and fire wheels (hoops bound with tow and soaked in pitch, which were ignited and rolled down onto the enemy). Piquancy was added to the situation by a trebuchet named 'The Tribute', probably in reference to the Turkish demand that a tribute be paid to them. Throwing machines had become an anachronism by 1480, and only Juan Aniboa, a Basque sailor, knew how to build this counterweight beam-sling engine. What did the defenders want a throwing engine for? They faced no shortage of cannon or powder. Most probably they were planning to bring plunging fire to bear upon concealed Turkish positions and had no mortars to implement this. However, no chronicle mentions whether the engine was successfully used.

Despite several unsuccessful landings at St Nicholas Tower, the Turks gave up trying to capture the outpost. They erected a huge siege tower on the opposite

Two Turkish 15th-century bombards. These or other similar cannon brought fire to bear upon the fortifications of Constantinople in 1453 and Rhodes in 1480. The rings on the sides of the barrels served for lifting and fixing the barrels. Before shooting, the barrel was laid onto an earthen embankment or a specially made wooden box.

G

side of the bay with a platform for archers and arquebusiers. The siege tower could not move, but from this excellent height fire could be brought to bear upon the defenders in St Nicholas Tower and on the mole. Unceasing bombardment of the tower began on 13 June and lasted for four days and nights. Under cover of this fire the Turks threw a great pontoon bridge across the bay wide enough for six men to march abreast.

The Turks undertook their first attempt to bring up the pontoon to St Nicholas Tower on the dark night of 17 June. The attack was foiled when the English sailor Roger Jervis heard the sound of muffled oars and bravely dived into water. He sawed the rope with which the pontoon was being drawn, and brought the grapnel to d'Aubusson. Roger was rewarded with a bag of gold.

The night of 18/19 June witnessed another Turkish attempt to seize St Nicholas Tower. At the same time as the pontoon was brought up, a fleet of 30 vessels, including galleys and store ships with cannon on board, approached the tower from the sea. Everything was accomplished in dead silence, so an alarm was sounded only when the pontoon was almost in position. Fabrizio del Carretto and his men slept in armour, weapons in hand. Quick though they were to take their positions on the alarm, the Janissaries were already advancing six men abreast along the pontoon and climbing up the debris of St Nicholas Tower, while disembarking irregular troops attacked the mole on the other side. At that moment the cannon of the French Post and those on the terrace of the Grand Masters' Palace opened fire. The artillerymen soon adjusted fire and a ball hit the pontoon breaking it into two. Many Janissaries fell into the water and drowned. The assault did not stop though. The Turkish landing troops rolled like waves upon the

Miniature from the manuscript of Caoursin. The outcome of the bloody battle fought at the walls of the Italian Post on 27 June 1480. The ditch is full of the bodies of defenders and attackers. In the background the Turks are breaking camp, burning the remaining structures. (MS lat. 6067, fol. 79r, Bibliothèque nationale de France)

G   THE SIEGE OF RHODES IN 1480

St Nicholas Tower was stormed on the night of 18/19 June. The tower was a key outpost of the city's defence. It commanded the entrance to Mandraki harbour and the approaches to the northern section of the city, where the Knights' quarter (Collachium) was situated. In the course of the siege of 1480 the Turks made numerous attempts to seize St Nicholas Tower. The night attack of 18/19 June 1480 was the most violent. On bringing up a pontoon from the opposite side of the bay, the Turks used it to assault the tower. At the same time 30 Turkish vessels approached the tower from the sea, opened fire and began landing troops.

A cannon ball launched by the defenders hit the pontoon and broke it in two. Many Janissaries fell into water and drowned. Meanwhile, the defenders brought out their fireships and directed them at the enemy fleet; four Turkish galleys and several transport ships were sunk. This, however, did not stop the assault. Turkish landing troops rolled in waves onto the ruins of St Nicholas Tower. The 57-year-old Grand Master Pierre d'Aubusson fought in battle shoulder to shoulder with the others, inspiring the defenders. A fierce battle lasted the whole night, and it was only by 10am on 19 June that the Turks retreated.

ruins of St Nicholas Tower, where hand-to-hand slaughter was now and then illuminated by the fire from guns, flaming arrows and the blasts of fire-pots. The defenders brought out fire ships and directed them at the enemy fleet. Four Turkish galleys and several store ships were ruined. Dramatic though the situation at St Nicholas Tower was, d'Aubusson transferred no reinforcements there from the Italian Post lest the latter be weakened. To make up for it, he personally took part in the battle for St Nicholas Tower, inspiring the men with his courage. He only just escaped being killed when a piece of cannon ball knocked his helmet off his head. The battle lasted all night, and the Turks only retreated at about 10am on 9 June. According to eyewitnesses, the sea was red with blood and for the next three days dead bodies were thrown up onto the shore. Misac Pasha spent those three days alone in his marquee refusing to see anybody.

Following their failure at this sector the Turks concentrated their efforts on the Italian Post. They succeeded in bringing a breaching battery close to the fortress walls and positioning it almost on the counterscarp of the ditch. By that time the walls of the Italian Post had already been turned into a heap of ruins, and only the Tower of Italy, partly destroyed, still rose above the rest of the fortifications. One dark moonless night, a detachment of Italian knights made a sally, sneaking along the ditch to attack the Turkish breaching battery. The knights spiked the enemy cannons, burned down wooden shelters and returned carrying the heads of Turkish artillerymen on their lances. However, their brave sally was incapable of changing the fact that a breach had already been made in the wall, and nothing could stop the Turks from storming it.

At dawn on 27 June the thunder of bombardment was replaced by an incredible noise coming from the Turkish camp. It was created by a mixed sound of pipes, cymbals and drum rolls. Misac Pasha ordered a black flag hoisted; this meant that the city would be given no quarter – it would be plundered and the inhabitants would all be killed or sold into slavery. As to the Hospitallers, they were to be impaled upon stakes. All this reached the defenders through letters fastened on arrows. The silence that followed was broken by a single cannon shot – the signal to assault.

Bashi-bazouks, irregular troops that knew nothing of discipline and served for booty, not for salary, formed the first storming wave. They were followed by Janissaries, who kept perfect order even under a shower of missiles launched from the Post of Provence. D'Aubusson realized that the ruined walls of the Italian Post could be held no longer – doing so would only lead to great losses. The defenders were therefore given order to retreat to the retrenchment. Engaged in the defence of the latter were most of the defenders, from crack units of the knights of each langue to members of the local population. The storming waves of the Turks rolled over the debris of the fortress walls and attacked the retrenchment. The Bashi-bazouks seized the Tower of Italy and fixed the Ottoman standard on it. It was a dramatic scene. Both sides desperately fought for the retrenchment, and 300 Janissaries penetrated into the city but were cut off from the main force and destroyed. Despite his declining years (he was 57) and an arrow wound in the hip, d'Aubusson together with a handful of knights led a counterattack on the wall-walk leading to the Tower of Italy, beat the Turks there and threw down the crescent of the Ottomans. His heroism cost the Grand Master dear: he was wounded four times, with one of the wounds particularly grave – a Janissary had broken through the breastplate of his armour with a spear and punctured a lung. D'Aubusson was rewarded for his efforts however – as he was carried away from the battlefield he saw the Bashi-bazouks turn around and take flight. The Janissaries tried to stop the retreat by killing the running Bashi-bazouks. It was at this moment that the defenders took the offensive. The outcome of the battle was decided. The Turks were fleeing and the battle turned into a slaughter. Led by the knights of all langues the defenders pursued the Turks up to their camp on the slopes of Mount St Stephen. They took the gold and silver standard of the Sultan and returned to the city, each carrying a Turkish head on a spear. Christian chroniclers assert that the Turks lost from 3,000 to 3,500 men in that battle; the figures, however, are in all probability overestimated, as is usual.

Ten days after the rout the Turks lifted the siege, boarded their ships and sailed away. When Sultan Mehmed II heard of the defeat, he flew into a fury and condemned Misac Pasha to death, though he later forgave him. Mehmed set about raising another army for the next year's campaign but he died on 3 May 1481. Because of dynastic problems facing his two sons and the changing political situation, the next invasion of Rhodes was put off for 42 years.

The city of Rhodes lay in ruin. Among the most damaged areas were the Jewish Quarter, the Grand Masters' Palace, the Italian Post and St Nicholas Tower. D'Aubusson commemorated the location of the battle for the Jewish Quarter by building a church dedicated to Our Lady of Victory there. Rhodians were relieved of taxation for the next five years. The Order of St John and the city of Rhodes received gifts from all over Europe.

The siege of Rhodes in 1480 demonstrated a transition from medieval siege methods to the gunpowder-based methods of the Renaissance. Artillery now played the main part in the siege, although elements of medieval siege warfare such as siege towers and trebuchets had not completely fallen into disuse.

1522

Nothing in the world was so well lost.

Charles V, Emperor of the Holy Roman Empire
(on the fall of Rhodes)

On 26 June 1522, a Turkish advance flotilla dropped anchor in Kalitheas Bay, some 10km to the south of Rhodes. From that day onwards, Turkish flotillas brought troops and equipment to the island for over a month – the last one arriving from Syria on 9 August. It was only on 28 July that Sultan Suleiman the Magnificent himself arrived on Rhodes. According to Christian chroniclers, the Turkish army numbered 200,000 men, of whom 60,000 were skilled miners (including many miners engaged by Suleiman in Bosnian and Wallachian territories famous for their masters). The figures are certainly overestimated, but there can be no doubt of the great strength of the Turkish army.

The Rhodian garrison consisted of about 2,000 men: 500 knights and sergeants-at-arms, 1,000 mercenaries and about 500 Rhodian militiamen. According to other data the garrison was from 5,000 to 7,500 men strong. The militia was formed on the basis of its members' position within Rhodian society; there was a Jewish detachment (the most numerous, containing 250 men), a detachment of butchers, and so on. During the course of the siege reinforcements of around 50 knights and 200 soldiers and sailors arrived. The city of Rhodes was provided with food and ammunition for a year of siege. As was done before the previous siege, all crops and gardens on the island were destroyed and buildings near the fortress walls were

The fortress of Rhodes in 1522

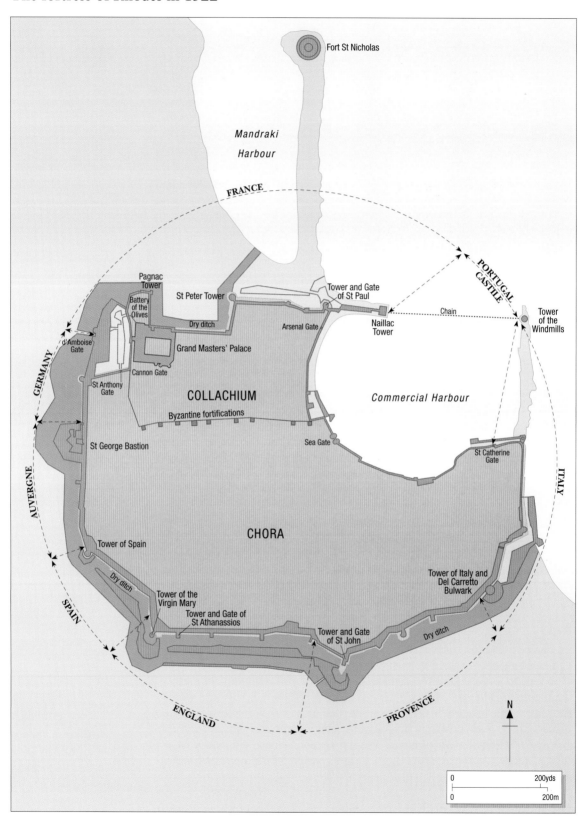

Fort St Nicholas

Mandraki Harbour

FRANCE

Pagnac Tower

Battery of the Olives

St Peter Tower

Tower and Gate of St Paul

PORTUGAL

CASTILE

Chain

Tower of the Windmills

d'Amboise Gate

Dry ditch

Grand Masters' Palace

Arsenal Gate

Naillac Tower

GERMANY

Cannon Gate

St Anthony Gate

COLLACHIUM

Byzantine fortifications

Commercial Harbour

St George Bastion

Sea Gate

St Catherine Gate

AUVERGNE

ITALY

Tower of Spain

CHORA

Tower of Italy and Del Carretto Bulwark

Dry ditch

SPAIN

Tower of the Virgin Mary

Tower and Gate of St Athanassios

Tower and Gate of St John

Dry ditch

ENGLAND

PROVENCE

N

0   200yds

0   200m

Two Turkish early 16th-century cannon. Such cannon brought fire to bear upon the Rhodes Fortress in 1522. Note that the bottom barrel, although dating from 1534, has been supplied with newly invented trunnions to allow the gunner to easily change the angle of the vertical laying.

demolished. Two great chains backed up by booms were thrown across the commercial port and hulks full of stones sunk in Mandraki harbour. Only a narrow channel was left navigable.

Having besieged the city on the mainland side, the Turks began to position their artillery. An eyewitness says that they had from 60 to 80 cannon of large calibre, 12 mortars and a great number of smaller cannon. The first large battery was put opposite the English Post, the second was aimed at the Spanish Post (each comprised four cannon of a very large calibre) and smaller batteries (consisting of two large-calibre cannon) were placed against other mainland posts. The Turks opened fire even before they had had time to dig in properly. The response they received was stunning – about half of the besiegers' cannon were put out of action by the defenders' fire. Nevertheless, the Turks continued bombarding the city. For a month, from the end of July to the end of August, 1,300 to 2,000 cannon balls fell on the city and its fortifications. The reported casualties were only 25 men killed (it is uncertain, however, whether common citizens were taken into account).

The day following the arrival of the Sultan, 29 July, saw the Turks digging trenches and mining galleries under the cover of a furious bombardment. The direction of the undermining was unclear, so Gabriele Tadini da Martinengo, a master Italian engineer in the service of the Order, suggested using 'mine detectors' – drums covered with parchment and hung with small bells. The strike of a miner's pick caused a slight vibration and the bells to ring; the louder they rang, the closer the undermining.

After ten days' bombardment of the German Post, under cover of night the battery was transferred from its original location to the foreshore opposite

Stone balls stuck in the walls of the Rhodes Fortress at the Italian Post. While restoring the fortifications, the balls were left in the wall as a reminder to posterity.

Fort St Nicholas. Attempts to destroy this outpost failed however. So, remembering their futile efforts here during the previous siege, the Turks thought it better to give up attempts on the fort and instead use these cannon to strengthen the batteries opposite the English and Spanish Posts. An earthwork towering above the fortress' walls was erected there, and artillery mounted on the heights silenced many of the defenders' guns.

By 14 August the bulwark and outworks of the English Post were seriously damaged. The walls of the Posts of Spain, England and Provence were soon breached. Fallen masonry filled the ditch and made an attack through the breaches easier. At night the defenders would restore fortifications, but the following day they were breached again. The defenders of the English and Spanish Posts suffered heavy losses from bombardment, so a mobile reserve was deployed here.

The walls of the Post of Italy were breached by 19 August, and on the same day Gabriele Tadini da Martinengo personally led 200 mounted knights and men-at-arms in a sally against the breaching battery placed opposite this post. The defenders killed many miners and destroyed a few cannon. Sallies were repeatedly made on 20, 22 and 24 August and each time the defenders returned bringing prisoners with them and carrying Turkish heads aloft on the points of their spears.

By September most of the walls on the mainland side were undermined with tunnels and the fortress walls were riddled with breaches, so a general storm was to be expected at any moment. To counter the underground mining Tadini dug out long tunnels along the mainland side from d'Amboise Gate to the Post of Italy. These tunnels ran perpendicular to Turkish tunnels and were to help the defenders discover and neutralize the latter. The first Turkish mine was detected under the Post of Provence and rendered harmless, but another one, which was not discovered in time, blew up on 4 September and the explosion under the bulwark of England shook the whole city and created a breach about 10m wide. A storming Turkish detachment assaulted through the ruins of the fortifications immediately, and managed to hoist their banners on the walls of the bulwark. Nevertheless, English knights fought desperately in a hand-to-hand battle and after two hours' fighting succeeded in throwing the enemy back to their positions.

Two more mines under the Post of Provence were safely neutralized on 9 September, but another mine under the English Post exploded, bringing down a stretch of masonry about 2m wide. The explosion was once again closely followed by an assault. Once more, a violent hand-to-hand action was won by the defenders, who even managed to seize a Turkish standard. However, their counterattack was a failure as the Turks positioned their sharpshooters on the counterscarp and forced the defenders to retreat, suffering heavy losses.

The day of 11 September saw new storming waves rolling onto the English Post and on 13 and 14 September two posts – the English and Spanish – were assaulted simultaneously. An attack on the Italian Post began on 20 September and was followed by simultaneous attacks of the posts of Provence, England and Spain. The Turks captured the Tower and bulwark of Spain and seized five Christian banners. In a fierce counterattack the knights recaptured the fortifications.

On 22 September, Tadini's miners rendered harmless a mine under the Spanish Post, but a mine under the Post of Auvergne blew up bringing down a part of the masonry. The wall was saved from complete demolition only by Tadini's series of 'spiral vents', through which the blast wave was directed outwards.

The fortress of Rhodes was most violently stormed on 24 September. At dawn the Turks opened fire with their cannon using specific gunpowder that produced black smoke to form a smokescreen. The defenders hardly had had time to realize where to expect the brunt of an attack when a crack Janissary detachment escaladed the walls and bulwark of the Spanish Post and stuck 30 or 40 banners there. After this first success a general assault began in the section from the Post of Spain to the Post of Italy. Despite the deadly fire brought to bear upon them, the Turks attacked bravely. Suleiman watched the battle from his seat on a raised platform. Grand Master l'Isle Adam was aged 57 at that time (he was then as old as d'Aubusson was in 1480) and appeared with his banner where the fighting was thickest. All Rhodians took part in repelling the assault; men fought on the walls, women brought them ammunition, food and drink and nursed the wounded. The desperate hand-to-hand battle lasted six hours and resulted in the enemy being beaten off the fortifications.

The bombardment of the city and attempts to undermine its fortifications continued throughout October and November. The Turks also attempted some unsuccessful attacks on the English and Spanish Posts. By October the knights of the English langue were all killed or disabled. The Frenchman Jean Bin de Malincorne was appointed commander of the Post of England and the ranks of its defenders were reinforced with knights from the other seven langues.

By December the city fortifications – particularly at the posts of Spain, England, Provence and Italy – lay in ruins. The townspeople were exhausted and on the verge of an insurrection and conclusion of their own peace treaty with the Turks. Stores of gunpowder and cannon balls had nearly run out. There was no more timber for the building of countermine galleries and no more workers to restore fortifications and transfer cannon from one place to another – all the slaves were either dead, wounded or sick. Citing Gabriele Tadini, the enemy was already in the city 'both above and below ground' (Brockman, p.149). Indeed, the Turks had developed an extensive network of underground galleries, which allowed them to appear in unexpected parts of the city. There

was no hope left of saving Rhodes, so when on 10 December 1522 Suleiman ordered a white flag to be shown and offered terms of capitulation, l'Isle Adam responded by flying the white flag on one of the towers of the Post of Provence, and accepted the offered terms. These were fairly mild: the Order and all its members were allowed to leave the island with all their property and weapons (with the exception of bronze cannon); the citizens' safety was guaranteed and they could either leave Rhodes together with the Hospitallers or within the following three years. Those who wished to stay on the island were granted freedom of religion.

After an agreement was reached, 25 knights and 25 prominent citizens were sent to the Turkish camp as temporary hostages. Then, 400 Janissaries entered the city while the rest of the Turkish troops were withdrawn to a distance of one mile (1.6km) from the counterscarp. Sultan Suleiman and Grand Master l'Isle Adam met three times and exchanged gifts. On 1 January 1523, the Hospitallers and those citizens that decided to join them sailed away from Rhodes. According to sources, the Greeks suffered in some unpleasant incidents after the Turkish army entered the city, but on the whole the Turks kept their promise, and marauders, to be found in any army, were punished.

The siege of Rhodes in 1522 is an excellent example of siege warfare of the Renaissance period. Medieval siege techniques and methods were no longer used. It was now based around gunpowder, which relies only on

View of the English (originally Aragon) Post. The ditch between the *tenaille* and counterscarp is littered with cannon balls – dumb witnesses of the Turkish siege of 1522. The English Post became the arena of the fiercest fighting during that siege.

The day of 24 September saw some of the bitterest fighting of the siege. At dawn the Turks opened fire with a special powder producing thick black smoke, which made a smokescreen. Before the defenders had realized where to expect an attack, a crack unit of Janissaries had already escaladed the walls and bulwark of the Spanish Post and hoisted nearly 40 banners there. The Janissary assault was followed by a general storm of the sector stretching from the Spanish to the Italian Post. The Turks attacked fearlessly regardless of the deadly fire coming from the defenders. Every citizen of Rhodes took part in the repulse; the men fought on the walls beating off the enemy, and the women brought them ammunition and food and drink and tended the wounded. After a fierce six-hour-long hand-to-hand combat the Turks were overcome.

artillery and mines. Where artillery was incapable of defeating the thick earthen walls of a new generation of fortifications, mines stuffed with powder were highly effective.

Like in the siege of 1480, the city was never completely blockaded in the siege of 1522. From time to time the Hospitallers received help that arrived by sea. On 9 November 1522, for instance, two brigantines came from Bodrum Castle. They brought 12 knights, 100 men-at-arms, and stocks of food and ammunition. On board two barques arriving from Lindos on 15 November were more reinforcements (12 knights) and munitions. These miserable reinforcements could not, however, change the general situation. No less than several thousand men were needed to save Rhodes.

The capitulation of Rhodes by no means proves that its defence was weaker than the assault. The fact that a handful of defenders resisted a vastly superior besieging force for as long as six months only shows that the fortifications of the city of Rhodes proved to be excellent. Had the Hospitallers received sufficient reinforcements from Europe, the fate of Rhodes could have been different.

Glass Turkish grenade discovered on Rhodes and supposedly dating from the siege of 1522. The grenade was filled with naphtha and thrown by hand. (Royal Artillery Museum, London)

AFTERMATH

On 1 January 1523, the 180 Knights Hospitallers who had survived the Turkish siege together with nearly 5,000 Rhodians boarded their ships and left Rhodes. After several years of wandering, the Order of St John found a new home in 1530. Acting at the Pope's request, Charles V, Holy Roman Emperor, granted the Knights of St John the islands of Malta and Gozo as well as the important city-fortress of Tripoli in Libya. The Order settled on Malta and waged successful wars against the Turks and against pirates until 1798, when Grand Master Ferdinand von Hompesch surrendered Malta to Napoleon I without a blow being struck. Rhodes was under Turkish control until 1912, when it was seized by Italy; in 1948 it became part of Greece.

The siege of 1522 caused extensive damage to the fortifications of Rhodes. Having seized the city, the Turks restored them but introduced no new defensive elements. In the subsequent centuries the fortifications gradually decayed as no noticeable effort was made to maintain them. Early in the 20th century the Italian administration began restoration works. Fortifications were cleared of the 19th-century Turkish buildings, and a number of gates, several towers, St George Bastion and some sections of the curtain walls were restored. Special attention was given to Fort St Nicholas, which was carefully restored.

The city of Rhodes and its medieval fortifications suffered from bombing in World War II. Moreover, to protect the harbour, Fort St Nicholas accommodated a battery of guns and machine guns, which changed the appearance of the old fort. Ever since Rhodes became part of Greece, the Greek Archaeological Service has been engaged in trying to return the fortifications to their original condition. Many sections have already been restored as high as the parapet.

The Turks used the Grand Masters' Palace as a prison. With no maintenance work being carried out, the building gradually fell into decay. Earthquakes that shook Rhodes from time to time did not assist in keeping the palace in good condition either. The final blow was struck in 1856, with the explosion of gunpowder stored in the neighbouring church of St John. The upper part of the palace fell down, and only the ground floor escaped destruction. An attempt to reconstruct the palace undertaken in 1937–40 by the Italian Governor of the Dodecanese C. M. de Vecchi is remarkable for its considerable lack of historical accuracy. Even some undamaged rooms on the ground floor were altered, and the upper part of the palace's appearance as it is now is the result of a purely arbitrary decision. Much history has been lost for ever.

The explosion of the church of St John also destroyed a number of buildings in the Street of the Knights, near the Grand Masters' Palace. The Turks built their own houses on the site. Under Italian sovereignty all Turkish structures were pulled down and houses in the 'Knightly' style were restored.

GLOSSARY

Abatis, abattis	A barrier made from felled trees with the sharpened boughs directed against the enemy.
Albarra	A detached tower brought forwards of a wall and connected with the wall by an easily removed bridge. This position provides a number of advantages: the effectiveness of the flanking fire from the tower is increased; the collapse of the tower does not cause the collapse of the curtain wall, and vice versa; and finally, if captured by the enemy, the tower can easily be isolated. This type of fortification is characteristic of the Iberian Peninsula.
Barbican	An outwork designed for the defence of a gate or a bridge leading to a gate.
Bartizan	A turret projecting outwards from the corner of a tower or wall on parapet level, used for observation and conducting flanking fire. Appearing in the High Middle Ages, they were quite common in Renaissance fortifications, but degenerated into decorative elements in later castle-like residences. They were typical of Spanish, Portuguese and French castles, and to a lesser degree of castles in other countries.
Bastion	A pentagonal structure of two faces, two flanks and an open gorge, directed towards the enemy at an acute angle. In the late 15th to early 16th centuries any projecting structure designed to enfilade a wall was called a bastion. It could be a round or square tower, or a circular or polygonal bulwark. Later, when a bastion proper was built, the name spread. Even now the term is sometimes used in a more general sense to include squat towers and bulwarks of various shapes. To avoid confusion the term bastion should only be used with reference to its final form – a pentagonal structure known also as an arrow-headed bastion. It is in this sense that the term is used in the book.
Bombard	From the Greek *bombos* (meaning 'droner' or 'rumbler'). A large-calibre cannon of the 14th and 15th centuries.
Bretèche	A small cabin or closed balcony projecting beyond the wall and supplied with one or several openings in the bottom. It fulfilled the same function as a machicolation, which was to make it possible to attack the enemy at the foot of a wall, but unlike the latter it was a very compact structure. A *bretèche* may have sat halfway up a wall or at the summit on parapet level, and

	may have been covered or open at the top. Extra loopholes were sometimes made in the front and sides of the cabin. A *bretèche* was often, but not always, placed above a gateway. In eastern fortifications *bretèches* were often placed only along the walls. Also known as a box machicolation.
Bulwark	A sizeable defensive work made from earth and some other material (such as wood or stone). In the artillery age the term shifted to apply also to bastion-like structures (polygonal or semicircular) built in front of some old fortifications. It is in this sense that the term is used in this book.
Bourga	*See* Chora.
Caponier	A covered defensive passage made in a dry ditch projecting away from the main *enceinte* in the direction of the enemy. It sometimes connected the main *enceinte* with outworks. It was chiefly designed for laying flanking fire along the ditch.
Chora	The southern, greater part of the city of Rhodes. *See* Collachium.
Collachium	The northern part of the city of Rhodes. It comprised the main buildings belonging to the Order of St John – the Grand Master's Palace, the Hospital, most important churches and the Knights' apartments. An inner wall separated Collachium from the southern part of the city (Chora or Bourga).
Counterscarp	The outer side of a ditch, often faced with stone.
Curtain	A wall between two towers or bastions.
Escarp	The inner side of a ditch. Sometimes, especially in the age of firearms, builders did without an escarp, raising a wall right from the bottom of the ditch.
Escutcheon	A coat of arms shield. In a special sense it can refer to an ornamental shield, made of stone or marble, fixed upon a fortress wall. It bore representations of coats of arms and other heraldic insignia.
Gabion	A cylinder-shaped wicker basket filled with earth.
Glacis	Smooth, gradually sloping ground outside a ditch. The slope has its highest point by the ditch and descends as it runs off the ditch. A glacis fulfills two important functions: it exposes the enemy and makes them an excellent target, and, owing to its elevated level, protects the lower part of the main *enceinte* from enemy artillery fire.
Machicolation	An overhanging structure on the battlement level of an arch or on stone corbels. Its bottom has one or several openings that allow the defenders to lay fire upon the enemy at the foot of a wall, or to throw down upon them various objects or pour liquids.
Mortar	A short-barrelled, large-calibre cannon that fires balls in a high, plunging trajectory.
Odos Ippoton	A local name for the Street of the Knights.
Outwork	Any defensive structure in front of the main *enceinte*.
Retrenchment	An inner line of defence erected beyond a breach made in the main defences of a fortress.
Talus	A sloping widening along the lower part of a wall or tower.
Tenaille	An outwork made in a ditch in front of a curtain.
Trebuchet	A counterweight beam-sling siege engine.

BIBLIOGRAPHY AND FURTHER READING

Andreev, A., Zaharov, V., Nastenko, I., *Istoria Maltiyskogo Ordena* (The history of the Maltese Order) (Moscow, 1999)

Brockman, E., *The Two Sieges of Rhodes: The Knights of St John at War 1480–1522* (New York, 1995). The richest study of the sieges of Rhodes of 1480 and 1522.

Caoursin, Guillaume, *The Siege of Rhodes* (New York, 1975). Unfortunately, this important source written by an eyewitness of the siege of Rhodes of 1480 is available only in the English translation made by John Kaye in 1482, so it can be read only with difficulty today.

De Curti, G., *La Città di Rodi assediata dai Turchi il 23 maggio 1480* (Venice, 1480)

Edwards, E., 'The Knights Hospitallers and the Conquest of Rhodes' in *The Proceedings of the Royal Philosophical Society of Glasgow*, 50 (Glasgow, 1918–20) pp.50–63

Fedden, R., *Crusader Castles: A Brief Study on the Military Architecture of the Crusades* (London, 1950)

Gabriel, A., *La Cité de Rhodes*, 2 vols (Paris, 1921 & 1923). The first serious analysis of medieval Rhodes and its fortifications. The first volume of the work, which can sometimes be found under the title *Les Ramparts de Rhodes, 1310–1522* (Paris, 1921), is devoted to the city fortifications. The work was the author's thesis for a doctor's degree. Even today A. Gabriel's work is the standard for the study of Rhodian fortifications. Unfortunately, it has never been translated into English.

Hale, J. R. (ed.), *The Early Development of the Bastion in Europe in the Late Middle Ages* (London, 1965)

Luttrell, Anthony, *Hospitallers in Cyprus, Rhodes, Greece, and the West 1291–1440* (London, 1978)

Luttrell, Anthony, *Hospitallers of Rhodes and their Mediterranean World* (London, 1992)

Riley-Smith, J., *Hospitallers: The History of the Order of St John* (London, 1999)

Rossi, E., *Assedio e Conquista di Rodi nel 1552* (Rome, 1927)

Kennedy, H., *Crusader Castles* (Cambridge, 2001)

Kollias, E., *The Knights of Rhodes: The Palace and the City* (Athens, 2003). An excellent guide to the fortress, the Grand Masters' Palace and other buildings of the city. Highly recommended for tourists.

Nicholson, H., *The Knights Hospitaller* (Woodbridge, 2001)

Nicolle, D., *Crusader Castles in Cyprus, Greece and the Aegean 1191–1571* (Oxford, 2007); *Knight Hospitaller (1) 1100–1306* (Oxford, 2001); *Knight Hospitaller (2) 1306–1565* (Oxford, 2001)

O'Malley, G., *The Knights Hospitaller of the English Langue 1460–1565* (New York, 2005)

O'Neil, J., 'Rhodes and the Origin of the Bastion', *The Antiquaries Journal*, vol. XXXIV, No. 1–2 (Cambridge, 1954) pp.44–54

Paradissis, A., *Fortresses and Castles of Greek Islands* (Athens, 1999)

Spiteri, S. C., *Fortresses of the Knights* (Malta, 2001). This is a revised, though abridged, version of *Fortresses of the Cross: Hospitaller Military Architecture (1136–1798)* by the same author published in Malta in 1994. I particularly recommend these wonderful books to those who are interested in research on Hospitaller castles.

INDEX

References to illustrations are shown in **bold**. Plates are shown with page and caption locators in brackets.